"As an author and consultant, I have seen firsthand the struggles that introverts face in a society built for extroverts. But I have also seen how powerful introverts can be once they embrace the gifts of a quiet and thoughtful temperament. In this deeply felt and beautifully reasoned guide for introverts in the church, pastor Adam McHugh shows the way for introverted Christians to find peace within themselves and their community."

Susan Cain, author of *Quiet: The Power of Introverts in a World That Can't Stop Talking*

"What a timely and badly needed book! *Introverts in the Church* will encourage thousands of Christians who have felt as if they don't quite fit. It will help them find their rightful place in Christian community, so that their gifts might be well used in the work of the kingdom. This book will also help churches to be a place where all people can flourish as disciples of Jesus. Adam McHugh has given us a precious gift through his openness, theological soundness and godly wisdom."

Dr. Mark D. Roberts, senior director and scholar-in-residence, Laity Lodge

"At last a book for and about introverts in ministry, and a wonderful book it is! McHugh unpacks the challenges and characteristics of the introvert leader in a ministry world designed for extroverts. He offers practical guidance for developing as a leader, evangelizing, joining a community, preaching and becoming spiritually mature in Christ. The book not only helps introverts, but it can serve as a great resource for extroverts who lead, coach, mentor or relate to introverts."

MaryKate Morse, author of *Making Room for Leadership,* and an introvert

"As an introvert who has experienced both the strengths and weaknesses of my temperament, I appreciate the way McHugh goes well beyond the facile stereotypes and conclusions of armchair psychologists. If you've ever felt vaguely sinful for not being a gregarious Christian I suggest you spend some quality time alone with a copy of *Introverts in the Church*."

Don Everts, minister of outreach, Bonhomme Presbyterian Church, Chesterfield, Missouri, and author of *I Once Was Lost*

"For the longest time, I've considered my wiring as an introvert a thorn in my side. After spending time engaging with others, I felt so empty and overwhelmed . . . and lonely. With my calling as an author and pastor requiring me to publicly speak and consult, I wondered if I misunderstood my place in this world. In *Introverts in the Church*, Adam brings a voice to those of us who often trade ours in for a little bit of respite. This is not only a needed resource for introverts; all leaders need to read *Introverts in the Church* for a better understanding of how introverts can lead, how they follow and how they refresh."

Anne Jackson, pastor, blogger and author of *Mad Church Disease: Overcoming the Burnout Epidemic*

"This is a book that all leaders in the church should read! It made me realize that I owe an apology to all the introverts whose insights and contributions I have not understood or have overlooked. McHugh's perceptions are crucial for churches in our extremely extroverted society—we are missing some of God's best treasures for Christ's body. I highly recommend this book to everyone who wishes more thoroughly to understand the Holy Spirit's creation of a diversity of personalities and gifts."

Marva J. Dawn, teaching fellow in spiritual theology, Regent College, Vancouver, British Columbia, and author of *My Soul Waits, Keeping the Sabbath Wholly* and *In the Beginning, GOD*

"Adam is addressing a huge number of folks in the church. Read it and heal."

John Ortberg, author and senior pastor, Menlo Park Presbyterian Church

A DAM S. M C H UGH

Introverts
in the
Church

FINDING OUR

PLACE IN AN

EXTROVERTED

CULTURE

IVP Books

An imprint of InterVarsity Press
Downers Grove, Illinois

InterVarsity Press
P.O. Box 1400, Downers Grove, IL 60515-1426
World Wide Web: www.ivpress.com
E-mail: email@ivpress.com

InterVarsity Press® is the book-publishing division of InterVarsity Christian Fellowship/USA®, a
movement of students and faculty active on campus at hundreds of universities, colleges and schools
of nursing in the United States of America, and a member movement of the International Fellowship
of Evangelical Students. For information about local and regional activities, write Public Relations
Dept., InterVarsity Christian Fellowship/USA, 6400 Schroeder Rd., P.O. Box 7895, Madison, WI
53707-7895, or visit the IVCF website at <www.intervarsity.org>.

Some names or details have been changed to protect the privacy of those involved, and some
characters are composites of two or more people—though all the stories told here are true.

Design: Cindy Kiple
Images: white church: Russell Shively/Shutterstock
          woman standing by the ocean: Lesley Aggar/Trevillion Images

ISBN 978-0-8308-3702-1

Printed in the United States of America ∞

Library of Congress Cataloging-in-Publication Data

McHugh, Adam S., 1976-
   Introverts in the church: finding our place in an extroverted
   culture/Adam S. McHugh.
       p. cm.
   Includes bibliographical references.
   ISBN 978-0-8308-3702-1 (pbk.: alk. paper)
   1. Introversion—Religious aspects—Christianity. 2.
   Introverts—Religious life. 3. Personality—Religious
   aspects—Christianity. 4. Psychology, Religious. I. Title.
   BV4597.58.I58M34   2009
   248.401'9—dc22
                 2009026587

P   22   21   20   19   18   17   16   15   14   13   12   11   10   9   8   7   6   5   4

Y   27   26   25   24   23   22   21   20   19   18   17   16   15   14   13   12   11   10

For Lindsay,

my favorite extrovert,

and

for all the introverts of faith

who inspired this book

and are gifts to the church.

Contents

INTRODUCTION

Can Introverts Thrive
in the Church?

Can introverts thrive in the church? This question goes beyond theology or psychological curiosity, and strikes me first on a deeply personal level. I am an introvert, and this question has fueled a meandering and bumpy journey that has led me in and out of Christian community, both as a layperson and as a pastor. This has been a journey of both self-discovery—as I have been learning how to make peace with my personality and to work out of it instead of against it—and of God-discovery—as I have been growing in my ability to see God's hand in my introverted life and ministry. On this journey I have been regularly accompanied by disappointment and hope, two companions that have worked together to push me onward.

•   •   •

I stand at a mailbox on a street corner in Princeton, New Jersey. As I stare at its familiar blue color, I wear only one winter glove, because the other ungloved hand clutches an envelope. It is a brisk afternoon, with the late winter winds gusting, negating the effects of the sun. New Jersey commuters, hoping to find a nonexistent short cut through the married-seminary-student neighborhood, pass by me with puzzled glances at this scene.

It is the day that my potential for leadership in the Christian community has come to an end, without ever truly beginning. What I hold in my ever-reddening hand is my resignation letter from the ordination process of my denomination. I have wrestled mightily with this process for four years, and just an hour earlier, I had resolved that I am not called to ordained ministry.

When I entered seminary, I had dreams of doctoral work in New Testament studies and a romanticized version of academia: I pictured myself sipping French roast and poring over the pages of my Greek New Testament with delight, attending snobbish cocktail parties and teaching eager students while wearing a tweed jacket with leather patches. Those hopes were dashed on the first warm spring day of April. When I was outside, relishing the rebirth of spring, all the Ph.D. students were sitting at their personalized library carrels, reading dusty books like every other day. I knew then as I reveled in the sunshine that scholarship was not for me.

So, as a fallback plan, I considered ordained ministry. Though I doubted whether I was well suited for such a ministry, I wondered what other career options a seminarian had. I squirmed through my classes on marriage and family, pastoral counseling, and spirituality and small groups, because pastoral ministry requires a person to move quickly in crisis situations, to float from one circle to the next, and to mobilize people of contrasting personalities. In other words, I knew that ordained ministry required social skills, and I wasn't sure I had them. Even when I was able to muster enough energy or warmth to connect with people, I was soon drained and exhausted, ready for a nap.

My one hope for pastoral ministry was that my teaching and preaching abilities would mitigate my questionable social skills. The events preceding this afternoon at the mailbox cracked that illusion. At my apartment a block away are the remnants of a blue test booklet, smoldering in a trashcan, which contains the ashes of my biblical exegesis exam, part of the strict regimen prescribed for ordination. Just a month earlier I had written an exposition of a passage in Matthew's Gospel and a sermon outline. But on this ungracious day, I have learned that I, a student in a New Testament master's degree program, have failed the biblical exegesis exam . . . again. It's time to go postal.

After receiving this knockout blow, I stroll up to the cold post office box, which will soon become the coffin for my vocational plans. I remove my glove, extract the resignation letter from my pea coat, and extend my hand toward the mailbox's jaws of death. But then I stop. Against the sagest of motherly advice, I stand in the frigid air, with my hand exposed, while the envelope flutters in the wind. Questions flood my mind: *Is it worth it? Do I really want to give up my future in ministry with this last impersonal act of defiance? Will I regret this hollow victory for the rest of my life? Is this more of an identity struggle than a career struggle? Am I letting my personal sense of failure and inadequacy preemptively disqualify me from pastoral ministry?* After about thirty cars pass, I turn, put on my glove and trudge home.

What had prevented me from slamming the mailbox door on my future in ministry? I'm not sure. But I do know that this story is unfinished.

•   •   •

Eight years later, I have come to realize that my death matches in those days were not *vocational* per se but were primarily *temperamental.* Even before I began pastoral ministry, I was convinced that my personality excluded me from it. There was no room in ministry for someone of my disposition—or so I thought.

In my mind at the time, ideal pastors were gregarious, able to move through crowds effortlessly, able to quickly turn strangers into friends. They could navigate diverse social circles and chat about any number of topics. They thrived in the presence of people and were energized by conversation and social interaction. Though they could work alone, their pulses quickened when they mingled among the people of their communities. They were charismatic and magnetic, capable of drawing all kinds of people to themselves by virtue of their likeability and able to persuade people to follow them based on charm alone. I saw them surrounded by eager church members, percolating with warmth, streaked with the admiration of their community.

I, by way of contrast, relished times of solitude, reflection and personal study. I enjoyed people, and I found satisfaction in depth of relationship and conversation, but even when I spent time with people I liked, I looked forward to moments of privacy. I found crowds draining. I could stand up in front of hundreds of people and preach a sermon without nervousness, but I often stumbled through the greeting time afterward because my energy reserves were dry.

Though I did not know this eight years ago, there is a label for this personality feature that I once thought crippled my potential for ministry: *introversion*. But more than my introverted temperament was involved in producing such agonizing doubts. Partly to blame was the one-dimensional image of leadership that I had constructed. There was an irresolvable conflict between that artificial image and the temperamental characteristics of introverts, and I subconsciously believed that ministers and other Christian leaders needed a certain set of personality traits in order to thrive in ministry. I tried to beat and squeeze myself into a mold of leadership instead of becoming the kind of leader that God designed me to be.

My struggles to be an introverted pastor are representative of the struggles many introverts face when navigating the waters of Christian community, which can be unintentionally, or intentionally, biased toward extroversion. As a pastor who has participated in both independent and denominationally affiliated churches, it is my experience that evangelical churches can be difficult places for introverts to thrive, both for theological and cultural reasons. Just as I have had a difficult time squaring my own temperament with common roles and expressions of the pastoral ministry, so also many introverted Christians struggle with how to find balance between their own natural tendencies and evangelical perspectives on community and evangelism. A subtle but insidious message can permeate these communities, a message that says God is most pleased with extroversion.

Fortunately, disappointment has not been my only fellow traveler on this road, but I have also been accompanied by hope: hope in the calling, healing and transformative power of God. My journey has not been guided by my own heroism or impressive displays of faithfulness, but by God's sovereignty. The same mysterious force that seemed to prevent me from depositing my resignation that day has also been a constant voice calling me into church ministry, parachurch ministry and chaplaincy. God is bringing me through a process of self-acceptance, both in terms of my introvert identity and also in terms of the gifts and contributions I bring to the Christian community.

My hope is that, through this book, God will begin or continue a process of healing introverts—helping them find freedom in their identities and confidence to live their faith in ways that feel natural and life-giving, the way that God intended. I want introverts to embrace that "you are no longer strangers and aliens, but you are citizens with the saints and also members of the household of God" (Eph 2:19). Further, I hope that God will unlock in introverts the tremendous gifts that they have to bring to the church. As I will discuss later, introverts have a set of qualities that contribute widely to the ministry of the church and to the building up of the body of Christ. When the church is led by introverts and extroverts who partner together, each contributing their strengths and offsetting the others' weaknesses, it is a testimony that the Holy Spirit is orchestrating the community, that it is not being run by the cult of personality.

I have only taken a few steps on this introverted journey of faith, but I wish to invite you, who are perhaps wearing only one glove yourself, to join and walk with me.

1

The Extroverted Church

"The extrovert God of John 3:16 does not beget an introvert people."

RICHARD HALVERSON, *THE TIMELESSNESS OF JESUS CHRIST*

In a 2004 psychological study, students at a Christian college were asked to rate the person of Jesus according to the profiles of temperaments in the Myers-Briggs Type Indicator. In most categories the students were divided, and they predictably showed a tendency to cast Jesus in their own image. But there were two categories in which students definitively came down on one side. In the thinking/feeling category, 87 percent of the students rated Jesus as a feeler; however 83 percent of the students also identified themselves as feelers. The truly revealing results, though, were found in the extrovert/introvert category. Although more than half (54 percent) of these students tested as introverts, most of the students surveyed (97 percent) said that Jesus was an extrovert.

Extroverts and introverts alike *overwhelmingly considered Jesus to be an extrovert.* This is surprising because the evidence of Jesus' personality is not clear-cut. Our Bibles that print his words in red tempt us to see him as a talking head, while relegating other aspects of his ministry to incidental circumstance. Though he regularly taught throngs of people, we also see him at critical times retreating from the crowds to pray in solitude and to spend time with his closest friends. He commandeers boats in order to create distance from the urgent demands and hectic energy of the people. He seems to prefer depth of relationship and conversation with a select few. While it is impossible to know for certain, Jesus' personality actually seems balanced between extroversion and introversion. How then does 97 percent of a focus group categorize Jesus as an extrovert? The psychology professor administering this study ventured an explanation and described its impact on introverts:

> The perception of an extroverted Jesus might reflect a tendency within American culture to value extroversion over introversion. If one assumes extroversion to be better, one might conclude that Jesus, the perfect human being, would have been an extrovert. . . . Making an assumption that Jesus was extroverted based on a cultural bias might make it difficult for introverts in such a culture to accept and affirm their own behavioral preference as legitimate and valuable; not something to be overcome or even tolerated, but something to be appreciated and blessed. Such an assumption might also make it easier for extroverts to overlook the strengths of introversion and the benefits introverts bring to their interactions with others.[1]

If human perfection, epitomized in the person of Jesus, includes extroversion then a large number of the population will always and irredeemably fall short. This adds a theological component to the already-prevailing cultural prejudice that extroversion is the superior temperament. In mainstream American culture (in schools, corporations and social institutions), those who are talkative, outgoing, energetic and assertive have a decided advantage. People who enjoy reflection and solitude, and listen more than they speak, are often viewed as enigmatic, antisocial and passive.

Marti Olsen Laney, who wrote *The Introvert Advantage*, says that "We live in a culture that caters to and extols extroverts. We definitely learn that extroversion is the way we *should* be."[2] She quotes David Myers, the author of the book *The Pursuit of Happiness*, who asserts that there are three essential ingredients in the recipe for happiness: self-esteem, optimism and extroversion.[3] He finds that, on the whole, extroverts are happier than introverts. Because of this bias, Jonathan Rauch, writer for *The Atlantic*, once dramatically stated that introverts are "among the most misunderstood and aggrieved groups in America, possibly the world."[4]

For decades psychologists and sociologists have cited findings that introverts comprise a quarter to a third of the general population, and they assumed that the struggles of introverts were intertwined with their minority status. Yet those findings were based on research done in 1962; more comprehensive personality surveys, done in the last ten years, have actually revealed that introverts are in the statistical majority at 50.7 percent of the population![5] And researchers point out that there are *not* more introverts in the population than there were in 1962, but our current data and samplings are just more thorough and accurate.

The slant toward extroversion in the larger culture has also infiltrated the church. I interviewed dozens of introverted Christians, and without exception, they expressed some degree of frustration and sense of exclusion from their churches. Many have found that their churches, in both theology and practice, are not accommodating to people of their temperament. These introverts have difficulty finding a place in their communities where they feel encouraged to be who they are and to serve in a way that is consistent with their nature.

For several years, my introverted friend Emily participated in a Christian community where extroversion was normal. Hailing from Japan, Emily was accustomed to a culture where deference to others and servanthood were considered highly desirable qualities, and she felt displaced in an American culture that valued self-promotion and aggressiveness.[6] She had positive relationships with people in the community, but she was always considered to be on the fringe because she spent a lot of time to herself. The ideal of "intimacy" in this community was people constantly together, and the implicit assumption was that the more activities and social interaction a person engaged in, the closer she was to God. Others thought Emily was antisocial and, therefore, lacking in faith. She was also resistant to sharing intimate details of her life with others, and her lack of vulnerability was construed as a heart resistant to God. Even though she had strong leadership traits, she was never asked to be a leader because she did not show the outward expressiveness that was considered a mark of faithfulness in this community. To her, the expectation to share everything with others felt intrusive, and she groaned, "Why do I have to let everyone into every corner of my life?"

THREE EVANGELICAL THEOLOGICAL ANCHORS
American partiality toward extroversion infects many Christian traditions, but certain church cultures are more difficult for introverts to navigate than others. I have found that features of evangelical church culture, even the defining attributes that comprise evangelicalism, can create environments that are intimidating and unnatural for introverts.

A disclaimer: In the pages that follow, I will admittedly be painting with broad strokes, and not every church or tradition will relate to all aspects of my critique of mainstream evangelicalism and its slant toward extroverted ways of thinking and acting. When the scales are weighted heavily on one side, as I believe evangelicalism is toward extroversion, we sometimes need to overemphasize a point in order to restore balance. In the same way, in portraying the characteristics and gifts of introverts, and what we have to offer evangelical churches, I do not presume to capture all the complexity of each individual introvert. Lastly, as I describe the qualities of introverts, I am not thereby implying that extroverts are *not* capable of those things (such as thoughtfulness or depth). In fact, as I will discuss in chapter two, each person has both an introverted and an extroverted side, though most of us will land on one side of the spectrum.

However, in most evangelical circles, there are three theological anchors—an intimate relationship with God through Jesus, the authority and centrality of the Bible, and active personal evangelism—that are often expressed in strikingly extroverted ways.

A personal relationship with God. At the heart of evangelical theology is the doctrine that God is personal. God is *intra*personal, in that his very being is composed of three separate persons who live in a dynamic state of mutuality, love and togetherness. Early church theologians used the word *perichoresis* (Greek for "dance") to describe the interconnectedness that characterizes the life and work of the three persons of the Trinity. God is also *inter*personal, in that he relates with his creation and seeks relationship with each one of his creatures. Evangelicals place central emphasis on the second person of the Trinity, the Son of God who appeared in human form as Jesus of Nazareth. We affirm that God's redemptive plan centers around the saving death of Jesus, and people receive the victorious power attained in his resurrection through a trusting, intimate, personal relationship with the living, ascended Christ. This Jesus is fully accessible to us and we can relate to him as a friend in open, informal and conversational interaction.

The evangelical priority on this kind of personal relationship with Jesus has direct implications for the nature of the community that forms around him. It is not surprising that evangelicals have a high value for intimate, informal relationships with one another, and we structure our churches—with small groups in our houses, fellowship hours, social events, accountability groups and prayer chains—in order to support this value. Most evangelical churches strongly encourage (and sometimes require) participation in these kinds of activities.

Unfortunately, sometimes our value for community life can become a substitute for relationship with God. Psychology professor Richard Beck says that for some churches *spirituality* is equated with *sociability*.[7] The mark of a progressing faith is familiarity with a growing number of people and participation in an increasing number of activities.

Yet for introverts who are wearied by and sometimes apprehensive of large quantities of social interaction, these evangelical emphases can feel discouraging and marginalizing. By no means are introverts against intimate relationships; indeed we are motivated by depth in our relationships. And while the emphasis on intimacy with Jesus is welcome, in community we prefer interactions with smaller numbers of people with whom we feel comfortable. So when an evangelical community explicitly or implicitly preaches broad interaction across the congregation, the introverted resistance to it can produce interior feelings of spiritual inadequacy.

Centrality of the Bible. Evangelicals are, perhaps, best known for their reverence for Scripture. The community is guided by, and shaped around, its interpretation of the Bible and its application to the governance, values and life of the community. Other church traditions also rely on ritual, symbolism, liturgy and iconography, but evangelicalism predominantly exalts the power of the Word. Evangelicalism is a self-proclaimed "word-based" community. Though throughout Scripture the "word of God" refers to different self-expressions of God, including the embodied Word in the person of Jesus, in evangelical churches the "word of God" is most used to describe the Bible.

Evangelical church services usually are organized to feature the sermon, in which the pastor routinely exposits a biblical text or texts. In some evangelical churches, the sermon may take more than half of the worship service. At the eight nondenominational, evangelical churches that I visited while writing this book, the sermon averaged forty-three minutes, and the entire worship service averaged eighty-one minutes. Sermons were intentionally delivered in a conversational and a loosely organized way, which contributed to their length. This style both emphasizes the centrality of Scripture in those communities and the regard for personal relationships that I have already mentioned. The pastors sought both to exposit Scripture and to connect on a personal level with their congregations.

This regard for the Bible and the informal preaching method of many evangelical pastors filter down into congregations and combine to create a conversational culture, in which learning about, discussing and living by the words of Scripture is very important. A love for the Word of God easily translates into a love for words about God . . . and words in general. Put more bluntly: Evangelicals talk a lot.

Former-evangelical-turned-Catholic-priest Thomas Howard explains a difference between Catholic practice and evangelical practice: "Emotionally, one would have to say that evangelicalism is a much more 'up front' form of piety, and very talkative."[8] Whereas in some church traditions you enter a sanctuary in a spirit of quiet reverence, in evangelical churches you walk into what feels like a nonalcoholic cocktail party. There is a chatty, mingling informality to evangelicalism, where words flow like wine.

To participate in the evangelical church is to join the conversation. Introverts, however, spare our words in unfamiliar contexts and often prefer to observe on the fringe rather than engage in the center. Our spirituality may be grounded in Scripture, yet is quieter, slower and more contemplative. In an upfront, talkative, active evangelical culture, we can be viewed as self-absorbed or standoffish, and we can feel like outsiders even when we have faithfully attended a church for years.

Personal evangelism. Evangelicals place a high priority on personal evangelism. We take Jesus' Great Commission—where he gave his followers the mission to announce God's kingdom—very seriously. An important part of our personal discipleship is sharing the good news with others. Typically, the evangelical emphasis has been on *speaking* the gospel. The famous line, attributed to Saint Francis: "Preach the gospel at all times—if necessary use words," has not traditionally been the backbone of our evangelistic methodology.

Instead, we believe that people come to know Jesus through conversation with those who already know him, through people who can persuade with relevant arguments or share their testimonies of God's goodness. This evangelistic style is consistent with the features of evangelicalism noted above, and evangelism is believed to be most effective when words are exchanged in the context of personal interaction. Some even teach that a true "evangelistic" interaction requires a thorough, verbal presentation of the gospel. At other times, evangelical evangelistic strategies are aggressive and confrontational. Some consider it our duty to challenge and disprove the viewpoints of others, simultaneously demonstrating the superiority of our worldview.

Apprehensiveness toward evangelism is not unique to introverts, but introverts may have a stronger resistance to evangelical methods for evangelism. A disinterest in small talk makes us reluctant to approach strangers, and we do not always have the energy to engage people in long conversation. Confrontation is not usually a comfortable approach for us, as our inner processing slows us down in a debate format. Our sense of personal uneasiness about evangelism is compounded by a spiritual guilt that creeps in when we fear we are neglecting the Great Commission.

Theological cornerstones of evangelical churches—like the accessibility of a personal, relational God, the authority and inspiration of Scripture, and the command to share the gospel and make new disciples—are paramount, indispensable values. Yet our methods for expressing those values are often tilted toward extroversion, and when we conflate our values with our methods we run the risk of alienating introverts.

HISTORICAL ROOTS OF THE EXTROVERTED CHURCH

The roots of the bias toward extroverted ways of thinking and acting reach back into the history of evangelicalism. The evangelical movement in the United States traces its origin to the Great Awakenings of the eighteenth and nineteenth centuries. The winds of revival swept through Europe and North America, bringing with them an eruption of conversions and rediscovered religious zeal. The Awakenings gave birth to fresh commitments of obedience to Scripture, and they were frequently accompanied by physical and emotional experiences of God's presence. People gathered for worship had personal experiences of God's holiness, and many collapsed into tears or froze in silent awe. Others fainted or trembled uncontrollably.

At the center of the first Great Awakening was George Whitefield, an English evangelist who preached in churches throughout the American colonies. Some people hiked for days to hear him, packing every venue. Church historian Mark Noll describes Whitefield's highly extroverted preaching style: "In the pulpit he simply exuded energy; his speech was to the highest degree dramatic; he offered breathtaking impersonations of biblical characters and needy sinners; he fired his listener's imagination; he wept profusely, often and with stunning effect."[9]

Even with these emotional displays, the first Great Awakening maintained a remarkable balance between heart and mind, owing largely to the genius and devotion of another prodigious figure of the time—Jonathan Edwards, an introverted, Congregationalist pastor in Massachusetts. He was able to provide an intellectual framework for the emotionally charged revivals, recording the movements of God in a short work called *A Faithful Narrative of the Surprising Work of God* and later penning a now-classic book that defended and clarified the nature of the revivals, *The Religious Affections*.[10]

During the Second Great Awakening—the origin of the camp meeting or tent revival—people would gather under a tent, sometimes for days on end, to hear evangelists preach the gospel. These evangelists addressed their listeners with dramatic urgency and intensity, impressing on them an immediate need for decision. People also responded with great emotion, sometimes in melodramatic displays of weeping or shrieking.

But whereas the first Awakening led to the founding of several of the country's most elite colleges, such as Princeton and Dartmouth, the Second Great Awakening of the late eighteenth and early nineteenth centuries introduced an anti-intellectual bent to evangelical Christianity. Suspicious of a dry, lifeless, academic faith, the leaders of the Second Great Awakening emphasized that conversion must be an *experience* in order to be authentic. Piety of the heart began to overshadow the understanding of the mind. A wedge was driven between the emotions and the intellect, a divide that would endure for generations of evangelicals. After the Second Great Awakening, many evangelical leaders eschewed learning and theological understanding altogether, to the point that nineteenth-century evangelist D. L. Moody boasted "My theology! I didn't know I had any!"[11] What mattered to them was a genuine inward devotion to Christ that expressed itself in a life of obedience.

Scholar Os Guinness explains that the tent revivals, the forebears of twentieth-century evangelical crusades, featured props and other innovations that were indicative of cultural pragmatism. Americans valued "hard work, common sense, ingenuity, and know-how" and did not have room or need for intellectual sophistication, abstraction or thoughtful reflection.[12] American evangelicals applied these pragmatic values to religion and began to focus on the visible effectiveness of their methods—in the form of tangible, quantifiable results.

Evangelicals today. Modern evangelicals are the heirs of the theology, values and practices of previous generations. We have received from our ancestors the bent toward piety and passion, as well as the tendencies toward anti-intellectualism and pragmatism.

Piety and passion. Evangelicalism continues to be primarily a religion of the heart. Personal piety can be beautiful and transformative, but sometimes our commitment to a "childlike faith" leads us to have an enthusiastic spirit that is intellectually and emotionally simple. Our historical roots in the Great Awakenings have led to an emphasis on overt, demonstrative, experiential displays of devotion.

This stress on public expressions of faith can set up a false model for what all "real" spiritual experience should look like, and it contributes to our evangelical verbosity. Henri Nouwen's words about this are sobering: "Sometimes it seems that our many words are more an expression of our doubt than our faith. It is as if we are not sure that God's Spirit can touch the hearts of people: we have to help him out and with many words, convince others of his power. But it is precisely this wordy unbelief which quenches the fire."[13] Sometimes words are a verbal mask for a spiritual void.

We might say that modern evangelicalism has a hearing problem. We often preach before we seek to understand a situation or before we sit in prayerful silence. Our verbal effusiveness can devolve into breezy clichés, hollow sound bites and repetitive song lyrics, things that don't honor the uniqueness, complexity and beauty of each person.

Anti-intellectualism and pragmatism. Though the intellectual climate of evangelicalism is changing, many remain skeptical of the role of the mind in Christian faith and are suspicious of academia and elite learning institutions. Mark Noll summarizes this part of evangelical culture: "To put it most simply, the evangelical ethos is activistic, populist, pragmatic, and utilitarian. It allows little space for broader or deeper intellectual effort because it is dominated by the urgencies of the moment."[14]

The pragmatism that we have inherited fosters an action-oriented culture. Evangelicalism values the doer over the thinker. The evangelical God has a big agenda. It's as if the moment we surrender our lives to Christ we are issued a flashing neon sign that says "GO!" There is a restless energy to evangelicalism that leads to a full schedule and a fast pace. Some have said that, in Christian culture, busyness is next to godliness. We are always in motion, constantly growing, ever expanding.

I'll never forget the statements a senior pastor of a 300-member congregation uttered when I interviewed for an associate pastor position: "This is a really high-octane environment. We're looking for someone who is excitable and high energy. You have to be totally sold out to work here. We work full throttle."

I double-checked my surroundings to make certain I was at a church and hadn't stumbled into an interview for the pit crew at the Indianapolis Speedway. I would have laughed at his statements if I wasn't so mortified. I was reminded of Eugene Peterson's indictment of our brand of Christianity: "American religion is conspicuous for its messianically pretentious energy, its embarrassingly banal prose, and its impatiently hustling ambition."[15]

The innovativeness of evangelicals has shaped the landscape of American religious life in ways that testify to this motion, growth and expansion. We invented the religious twentieth-century landmark: the megachurch—an expression of the church that introduced the paradox of people worshiping together in anonymity. At its best, the church growth movement has reached thousands of people with the gospel and shrewdly connected with the surrounding culture. At its worst, it has produced a superficial, consumerist mold of Christianity that has sold the gospel like a commodity.

Many evangelical megachurches, in their hope to create comfortable environments for seekers, have stripped their sanctuaries and worship services of any sense of mystery and the sacred. Their fast moving, high production events may entertain us and their avid employment of modern technology may dazzle us, but many times, they cannot help us hear the still, small voice of God.

The megachurch has fed our American preoccupations with size and celebrity, and some of the largest implications have come for our models of leadership. At the center of most megachurches is a big personality: a dynamic, larger-than-life pastor who is able to hold everything together with his charisma. *Time* magazine and various Christian publications now release lists of the most influential evangelicals, so fame and stardom have crept into evangelical culture. As churches rush to imitate the success of others, they go for what they think is the guaranteed recipe for prosperity, starting with finding a pastor with big presence and star power. The description of George Whitefield above might be the description of the ideal candidate for an evangelical pastor—except for, perhaps, his profuse weeping from the pulpit.

Implications for introverts. Not all pastors of megachurches are extroverts, though a recent Barna study of 627 senior pastors of Protestant churches found that 75 percent of them are. And human limitations often lead to pastors forming congregations in their own image, presenting a picture of Jesus and of discipleship that matches their own patterns. It is not surprising then that extroverted pastors are prone to encourage extroversion in their churches.

Even introverted pastors, though, feel the pressure to act like extroverts. A well-known pastor of a large congregation acknowledged that social interaction drains him and that he prefers not to be in the spotlight. Yet the social demands of his job are staggering. He lamented that, in his congregation, he is expected to be the "lead socializer"—the first one on the church patio and the last one to leave. All the interviews I conducted with introverted pastors yielded one commonality: the coffee hour after worship is one of their least favorite hours of the week. They love their people, but after expending a tremendous amount of emotional energy to preach, they would prefer to disappear into their offices than mingle.

A therapist I know who frequently works with pastors said that many of her introverted clients struggle to find balance in their lives and often wrestle with depression. It seems that many introverts pay a high cost to be in ministry. They feel unable to meet the social expectations placed on them by their congregations, and they frequently lack adequate boundaries to enable them to find rest and to recharge their introverted batteries. Because of these challenges, one friend, who was part of a pastoral nominating committee, observed that the group's unspoken mantra was "if your personality starts with the letter 'I,' you need not apply."

All of these factors of mainstream evangelicalism combine to create an environment that can be marginalizing and even exclusive of introverts. For example, the up-front piety of evangelicalism, and the expectations for outward, emotional displays of faith, can feel invasive and artificial to introverts. Meanwhile, the anti-intellectual stream can alienate some introverted thinkers who find that their love of ideas, comfort in solitude and powers of concentration translate into a life of intellectual pursuits. Furthermore, the pragmatism that seeks measurable, tangible gauges for success strikes many introverts, who appreciate depth, as superficial and oversimplistic, and our action-oriented culture does not always value people who are thoughtful and reflective.[16]

THE INTROVERTED CHURCH

Versions of the word *introvert* are indelicately used in evangelical thought to refer to an ingrown, self-centered version of the church:

> An introverted church, turned in on itself, preoccupied with its own survival, has virtually forfeited the right to be a

church, for it is denying a major part of its own being.[17]

The extrovert God of John 3:16 does not beget an introvert people. There is a terrible tendency to make the gospel serve us, to use it as a protection against the realities of life as though Christ died to preserve the status quo.[18]

But the introverted church wants to secure the church doors against divine surprises and unannounced entrances by the King.[19]

The explicit and direct command [the Great Commission] to Matthew's Jewish readers may represent a challenge to their tendency toward introversion . . . the introversion that was an exception in the first century has now become commonplace in contemporary Western churches.[20]

To these writers and many others, "introversion" is equated with disobedience. In their minds, the "introverted" version of the church lacks a missional identity; it is self-preoccupied and exclusive, worried about polishing the walls that separate it from the world, rather than seeking to tear down the walls that distance people from the love of God. God the "extrovert" has his eye on all the world, and therefore the mark of his true people must obviously be extroversion.

Without doubt, the nature of the churches described by these quotations is a distortion of what Jesus had in mind when he called his followers to make disciples of all nations. A church that is self-focused and insular is a social club, not a church. While the authors are not referring to introverted individuals, to apply the term *introverted* to this kind of church is only to heap coal on the fire of an already-damaged introverted psyche. By way of analogy, imagine if we were to critique the church as soft, domestic and comfortable, and then we labeled it the "feminine" church. That would be insulting to women and to the feminine qualities in all of us. So to call the isolated church "introverted" only reinforces stereotypes that plague people who are properly called introverts.

Further, I'm not convinced that the "extroverted" church would be any more faithful to the biblical vision. If a church, turning away from self-protection and parochialism, committed itself to being an "extroverted" community, the opposite imbalance could easily occur. If we are broadly defining the extroverted church as "outwardly oriented," then a wholly extroverted church is liable to lose its center, lapsing into spiritual compromise and excessive cultural accommodation. Just as a church that is turned in on itself is stunted, a community that is thoroughly turned outward could lose its internal cohesion and disintegrate. Furthermore, as I will discuss, one of the ways we discover the compassion that lies at the heart of mission is to look inward. I believe that the truly healthy church is a combination of introverted and extroverted qualities that fluidly move together. Only in that partnership can we capture both the depth and breadth of God's mission.

Introverted ancestors. The marginalization of introverts in Christian communities is a relatively new phenomenon when we consider the history of the church. There have been many periods in which solitary, contemplative believers have been among the most esteemed figures. In the fourth and fifth centuries, a group of men and women retreated away from the wealth and ostentation of newly established Christendom—which was a far cry from the persecuted underground of early Christianity—and moved into the Egyptian desert. These spiritual refugees, known as the Desert Fathers and Mothers, lived in radical solitude to do battle with the forces of temptation and sin that besieged their souls. They sought unencumbered encounter with God through contemplation and unceasing prayer.

Even though these monastics (from the Greek word for "solitary") wanted to remove themselves from society, over time they became the conscience and the de facto moral leadership of the church. Eager apprentices from the cities followed them into their holes for wisdom and instruction, and even priests and bishops inquired after their counsel and blessing. Though they initially sought the isolated refuge of the desert, they came to understand their responsibility for teaching others, and they gave birth to monastic communities committed to spiritual discipline, work and mission. Through their devotion, they actually changed the ecclesiastical structures of the church. Formerly known for their eccentricity, the Desert Fathers and Mothers became revered for their holiness, humility and contemplative knowledge of God.

In our day, I am convinced that introverts are an important ingredient in the antidote to what ails evangelicalism. Our slower pace of life, our thoughtfulness, our spiritual and intellectual depth, and our listening abilities are prophetic qualities for the evangelical community, calling us to a renewed understanding of God and a fresh reading on the abundant life Jesus came to give us. Yet because of the extroverted bias in many of our churches, introverts are leading double lives. We are masquerading as extroverts in order to find acceptance, yet we feel displaced and confused. We are weary of fighting our introversion, and we long to live faithfully as the people we were created to be.

2

The Introverted Difference

"He is not a man that is easy to draw out, though he can be communicative enough when the fancy seizes him."

STAMFORD, DESCRIBING SHERLOCK HOLMES TO DR. WATSON,
IN SIR ARTHUR CONAN DOYLE, *A STUDY IN SCARLET*

"If I am to lodge with anyone, I should prefer a man of studious and quiet habits."

DR. WATSON, IN SIR ARTHUR CONAN DOYLE, *A STUDY IN SCARLET*

"I get in the dumps at times, and don't open my mouth for days on end. You must not think I am sulky when I do that. Just let me alone, and I'll soon be right."

SHERLOCK HOLMES, IN SIR ARTHUR CONAN DOYLE, *A STUDY IN SCARLET*

We all have two dead European psychologists dueling in our heads.

In the early twentieth century Sigmund Freud and his disciple-turned-rival, Carl Jung, clashed over the nature of introversion.[1] For Freud, introversion indicated an unhealthy self-preoccupation. It was a pathological step toward narcissism, a disorder that involves obsession with the self to the exclusion of others, a habitual turning away from the outside world.

The term *narcissism* originates from the Greek myth of Narcissus, who became enamored with his reflection in a pool of water. One day, when stooping to take a drink, he caught a glimpse of himself in the pond and was entranced by his image. He became so obsessed with his reflection that he turned away from others, spurning the women who loved him, including the nymph Echo who, after this rejection, withered away in caves until she became a mere whisper. Unable to consummate his love with his own image, Narcissus stood immobile over his reflection for so long that he became part of the environment and turned into a flower.

Narcissus rejected the world and the potential for fulfillment and healthy relationships, retreating into the gratification of his ego. Freud, therefore, chose the term *narcissism* to refer to this level of self-infatuation and world-rejection. In Freud's perspective, introversion was a dangerous step toward narcissism, as it was the beginning of an exchange of external reality for internal fantasy. In Freud's view, if introverts have not yet become infatuated with their own image, they are certainly bending down to take a drink.

Carl Jung, in contrast, considered introversion a healthy and normal trait. Part of his collective-unconscious theory, which concerns the general psychological patterns shared by humankind, introversion (a term he coined) was an introspective orientation, wherein a person finds primary energy within the self. Extroversion, on the other hand, is an outward orientation, where an individual finds primary energy outside of the self in the surrounding world. Instead of claiming, as Freud did, that these tendencies merely resulted from family background and social constructs, Jung argued that these psychological types were inborn. Whereas Freud posited a temperamental dichotomy of "normal" and "ab-

normal," Jung placed introverts and extroverts on an energy continuum, each being legitimate and healthy.

In psychology circles, Carl Jung has won the day. His collective-
unconscious theory is the basis of the Myers-Briggs Type Indicator
(MBTI), a popular personality inventory tool that breaks down
preferences into four categories of opposite pairs. The first pair is
introversion and extroversion.[2] Regarding introversion, there is
wide agreement that it is a normal phenomenon and healthy temperament, but in the minds of many introverts, the debate between
Freud and Jung rages on. Because our mainstream culture, even in
our churches, praises the virtues of extroversion, practically every
introvert has agonized with questions like "Is something wrong
with me?" The voices of others echo in our heads, sometimes with
a frequency and volume that drown out our own.

Introverts are targets for a variety of misguided arrows: we are
shy, reserved, aloof, reclusive, melancholic, self-absorbed, passive,
timid, social rejects, misanthropes and the list goes on. Psychologist Laurie Helgoe says that "we think of introverts as withdrawn
loners, quiet, and scared. We readily diagnose a preference for
looking inward as stemming from depression, anxiety, or antisocial tendencies."[3] But none of these are proper descriptions of the
introverted temperament; these are distortions that result from
others' misunderstandings or our own confusion.

DEFINING OUR TERMS

Introversion and extroversion do not describe categories of people
but two separate forces within each person. Each person has a
capacity for looking outward at the world of people, things, activities and events, as well as a capacity for searching inward in the
world of thoughts, feelings, imagination and ideas. All of our personalities move in these two directions. But while human personality is fluid and our personality types seem to ebb and flow depending on context and circumstances, most people tend toward

one side of the continuum. Introversion or extroversion is a *prefer-ence,* just like left- or right-handedness,[4] and we will favor one over the other to varying degrees.

Within introversion itself there is great variety. There is not an introverted mold, and as much as psychology helps us, it's impos-sible to distill the full complexity and mystery of human personal-ity into a list of characteristics. The degree our introversion is ex-pressed is determined, in part, by our family and cultural backgrounds. Further, Myers-Briggs lists eight different types of introverts, depending on how they score in the *other* personality categories (intuiting/sensing, thinking/feeling and perceiving/judging). Introversion is *one* of a constellation of factors that flu-idly work together to shape how we act. Introverts gather the in-formation that feeds our inner worlds in different ways; some rely on the concrete experiences of their senses (an S on the Myers-Briggs), while some depend more on their intuition (an N), inter-preting what lies below the surface. Some introverts make deci-sions more from their hearts (an F) and others more from their heads (a T). Some prefer to structure their lives carefully (a J), whereas others opt for more spontaneity and flexibility (a P).

Not all introverts will relate to every detail in the pages that follow. My own confession is that I score high on both the intui-tive (N) and thinking (T) categories of the Myers-Briggs, and while I interviewed many people who fall into the sensing (S) and feeling (F) categories, I am not always able to isolate my intro-verted traits from other parts of my personality.

Energy source. There are three primary characteristics of intro-version, and the first has to do with energy source.[5] Given that we live in a finite world and have limited amounts of energy, where and how do we refuel? Introverts are *energized by solitude.* We are recharged from the inside out, from the forces of our internal world of ideas and feelings. Just as a geyser finds its power from a subterranean water source, introverts derive strength from hidden places. We generally fill our energy tanks in private or in the presence of one or two close friends, or else in a public place without interacting with those around us.

Some people misconstrue the introverted need for solitude as being antisocial. But it's not that we don't *like* people, it's that time with other people in the external world has a draining effect on us. We don't avoid social situations like we would a trip to the dentist, but sometimes we avoid them like we might avoid exercise, because we lack the energy for it. Long periods without quiet refueling leave introverts feeling physically exhausted and emotionally hollow.

At a recent conference for college students, I had the opportunity to pray for a number of people during a time of worship. Students cascaded to the back of the room to receive prayer for deeply personal and sometimes agonizing identity, family and spiritual issues. I prayed for them with energy and compassion, but after about an hour and a half, as the stream of students flowed on, I was running on the fumes of my introverted fuel. My prayers became shorter and shorter and my words sluggish. I still looked like the same person, I still sounded like the same person, but somehow I wasn't. It was an introverted out-of-body experience. The room began to lose its shape, and I can hardly remember who I prayed for and what we prayed about in the last thirty minutes of the night. After the worship experience came to a close, the leaders gathered briefly. I vaguely remember lying down on three padded chairs and curling into the fetal position. The next morning my head pounded with the effects of an introverted hangover. I had overconsumed on external stimulation.

Extroverts, on the other hand, derive their energy from outside of themselves. They need other people, interaction and various kinds of stimulation in order to replenish their energy. They are like a reservoir that relies on rainfall for water. They are refilled by external sources. Too much time alone, silence or inactivity leaves extroverts feeling drained.

My extroverted friend Justin slowly spirals into depression when his housemates are out of town. At first he is filled with energy to accomplish neglected tasks around the house, but the solitude and quiet slowly taps his energy until, in his words, "I become weird and neurotic. All I can do is watch TV and play computer games, and I lose the ability to speak in full sentences." Whereas that describes my behavior if I have spent too much time with people, Justin needs social interaction in order to feel "normal."

It is important to differentiate between energy source and energy level. People sometimes think of introverts as listless or despondent, the Eeyores of the social scene. But it's not that we have less energy, it's that we lose it through interaction. We start to flag after an extended period without solitude. Depending on other personality and biological factors, we may charge to a high level, but we have a shorter battery life than extroverts. Further, many of us have learned to move and talk a little slower in order to preserve our social energy. Extroverts, likewise, can start with varying degrees of energy, even less than some introverts, but they will gain power from the outside world and leave with more than they came in with.

Internal processing. The second classic mark of introversion is internal processing. In our culture we are continuously bombarded by stimuli, in the forms of information, images, conversation, and a multitude of other data and experiences. In order for introverts' lives not to degenerate into disassociated states of confusion, we need to process these stimuli and integrate them into our lives. Another way that this integration process might be described is *filtering*. We need to filter information and experiences, allowing the good to take root in us and transform us, discarding the bad or irrelevant.

Introverted and extroverted filtration systems are different. Extroverts have flexible and porous filters that allow much to pass without getting clogged. They can usually take a much higher amount of stimuli before they become inundated. They mostly process externally, through conversation and interaction with others. Talking is an integral part of their processing, and they often speak in order to understand. Their speaking and thinking occur simultaneously. Though they are capable of internal filtering and reflection, they are most alive when engaged in the world of people and activity. This tendency lends itself toward a trial-and-error learning style, as they depend on external feedback to grow. Their outward filtering is done not only with words but also with their bodies, so extroverts may be more physically expressive than introverts.

The introverted filter, on the other hand, is much finer and more rigid, only able to allow small amounts of stimuli to pass before it backs up. Introverts process internally, in the workings of our own minds. We integrate and think silently. Ideally, we like to be removed from external stimuli and people in order to process. Our thinking precedes our speaking, which means we will often pause as we reflect and carefully choose our words. This tendency can be exasperating to some extroverts, who may find themselves wanting to finish our sentences. Though we are capable of engaging in the world, we are most alive in the reflections of our minds, mulling over concepts and experiences. Our learning style centers around observation and contemplation, and we are not as dependent on external feedback for growth.

Many introverts do not do well with interruptions, either when we are speaking or reflecting. Because we draw conclusions before speaking, interruptions disrupt our train of thought and force us to process newly presented information before responding. Introverts may become even more frustrated when people mislabel their internal processing:

One of the big mistakes Extraverts make is to assume that if someone is not engaged with another person, that individual is simply not busy. So, it's okay to interrupt someone sitting and reading because that person is probably reading only because there's no one else with whom she can talk. You can only imagine what an Extravert thinks of someone who is sitting there not even reading but merely *reflecting*. Clearly that person needs to be put to some more useful task—such as listening to the Extravert's thoughts of the moment.[6]

When the finer filters of introverts become clogged in the presence of people, we often go silent. Though we may appear composed on the outside, our minds are in a state of constant activity. When important or difficult information comes our way, ideas swirl in our heads in a hurricane of mental activity while our faces show no ripples. One friend, a pastor of a large Presbyterian church, said when she was young, she was surprised to hear her mother describe her as "quiet," because "it was *never* quiet in my head."

When this filtration process is impeded, the result can be disorientation and confusion—or for me, temporary depression, which is even more confusing because I can start attributing those feelings to spiritual causes or other sources. My introverted engine once dramatically broke down after two consecutive weeks of student conferences. The first week was a summer conference, filled with eighteen hours a day of Bible study, skits, staff meetings, group meals, pastoral interactions with students, virtually nonstop conversation and communal sleeping arrangements. It was a glorious week of seeing the work of God—and an introvert's nightmare. After this taxing week, we began a second five-day retreat, to reflect on the completed school year and to envision the upcoming year. All that I wanted to reflect on was the softness of my pillow.

Two days into this second retreat, my filter was thoroughly clogged, filled with the bitter, moldy "grounds" of the last week and a half, and I was in a full introverted malaise. External stimulation had triumphed over me. Though I managed to keep my composure during the day, at night in the safety of my apartment I fell apart. I spouted to my wife, "I'm not going back! I *hate* my job! I can't do this anymore! Why in the world did I take this job anyway? Why didn't you stop me?! What was God thinking anyway?!! Adam as a college pastor? Lunacy!" At 2 a.m. that night, as I walked through the apartment grounds, I seriously considered resignation.

It's amusing to look back on those moments of despair, when I was screaming "My God, my God why have you forsaken me?" I realize now that I was not experiencing spiritual disillusionment but simply introvert overload. Fortunately, I have a patient wife and friends who helped me through that time, prescribing rest and solitude.

I was also relieved when I recently discovered that other introverted ministers have had parallel experiences. Sean, a veteran youth minister, told his own story of leading a weeklong conference. He began his week full of energy, insight and compassion, but as the week grinded on, his balloon deflated. By Thursday he was impatient, tired and depressed. Little things began to gnaw at him, and what were gentle interactions with students earlier in the week became shorter and sharper. Unlike me, however, Sean was able to diagnose the source of his condition, and he avoided falling into despair. For him, this was not the onset of a "dark night of the soul" but merely a sign directing him toward an extended afternoon nap. Sometimes he would even check into a hotel for a night after a conference to avoid taking out the frustrations of his introverted overload on his family. For introverts, self-understanding can prevent disasters.

The combination of solitude and internal processing means that many introverts are more oriented toward ideas than they are interacting with people. We may be thinking *about* people, but we are often doing so while removed from conversation with them. Introverts (especially those who score high in the "thinking" category of the Myers-Briggs) treat our ideas like friends, devoting the same energy and time to them. Likewise, we consider books and authors as mentors, or as midwives to our most profound ideas. While extroverts may gauge their day by the quality of interactions and experiences they had, introverts often gauge their day by the thoughts and reflections they had. We may even enjoy reflecting on our experiences more than we enjoy the experiences themselves.

Depth over breadth. A third distinctive of the introverted temperament is the preference for depth over breadth. This applies to various aspects of our lives. Introverts tend toward high degrees of intimacy in our relationships, which we usually have fewer of than extroverts. Introverts are rarely content with surface-level relationships and do not generally consider our acquaintances to be friends. We may find small talk to be disagreeable and tiring. Because we often prefer to spend time in one-on-one interactions, rather than group socializing, our relationships can run deeper.

Introverts also prefer to have depth in fewer interests. This trait is connected to our style of processing. A breadth of information about a wealth of topics often results in introverted-filter overload. Instead, introverts prefer to invest our energy resources into a smaller number of topics or activities. We desire to mine them for all their richness, to explore all their nuances and complexities. This commitment to specialization of expertise, along with our love of ideas and our powers of concentration, explains why many introverts thrive in lives of scholarship.

Our passion for depth also applies to our understanding of ourselves. Whereas for extroverts, there may be no limit to the breadth of experiences and acquaintances they can have, for introverts there is no end in our journey of self-discovery. Introverts are experts in our internal worlds, aware of the strata of motivations, feelings and assumptions that determine our choices and behaviors.

Here is a summary of common attributes of introverts:

- Prefer to relax alone or with a few close friends
- Consider only deep relationships as friends
- Need rest after outside activities, even ones we enjoy
- Often listen but talk a lot about topics of importance to us
- Appear calm, self-contained and like to observe
- Tend to think before we speak or act
- May prefer a quiet atmosphere
- Experience our minds going blank in groups or under pressure
- Don't like feeling rushed
- Have great powers of concentration
- Dislike small talk
- Are territorial—desire private space and time
- May treat their homes as their sanctuaries
- Prefer to work on own rather than with a group
- May prefer written communication
- Do not share private thoughts with many people[7]

Because introversion is not synonymous with shyness or aloofness, true introverts are harder to identify than you might think. You can't always look for wallflowers or people staring at their feet to determine who the introverts are. Healthy introverts are not recluses. Just because we are oriented toward our inner worlds does not necessitate that we live in a *private* world, devoid of social contact and activity. It means that whatever context we are in, we are predisposed toward what is happening inside of us more than we are in what is taking place around us. Introverts can be in an unruly crowd, still immersed in our internal worlds.

Introverts can be elusive in social settings, depending on our comfort and energy level going into a situation. If you ask different people acquainted in various capacities and contexts with a particular introvert, you may get very different perceptions. Some might say he is cold and distant, but others might say he is warm and outgoing.

In most social situations with our close friends, I am usually among the crowd, laughing and talking, much closer to the center of attention. My wife, Lindsay, on the other hand, usually finds one or two close friends, sits in one place away from the action and has extended conversations with them. Most of our friends would say she is an introvert and I am an extrovert. But in situations involving strangers or acquaintances, I am either positioned at the fringes of the room or else sitting among a group of people listening and only infrequently contributing to the conversation. Lindsay, on the other hand, is floating through the room and striking up conversations.

Regardless of the social context, our true temperaments are always revealed in the trip home. Lindsay drives because I'm too exhausted. She wants to reenact her conversations and summarize what happened. This is the consummation of her experience. Meanwhile, I sit next to her with my eyes half open and my head firmly planted on the headrest. I try, usually unsatisfactorily, to make active listening sounds. I am either half asleep or else silently processing all of the interactions I have had. This is the completion of my social experience. My energy is depleted, while hers continues to build.

CREATED AS INTROVERTS

Introversion is not a mere social construct or learned behavior. There is increasing evidence that introversion is hard-wired into our brains, and that it appears at a very early age. Traditionally, psychologists have identified introversion by its behavioral patterns and symptoms, but with new technologies for mapping the human brain have come the understanding that introverted and extroverted brains work differently.[8] Our differing behaviors and tendencies are expressions of physiological and chemical variations. We not only exhibit introverted behaviors but we *are* introverts. Theologically speaking, we can say that we are *created* as introverts. When our Creator knit us together, he shaped our brains in such a way that we would find satisfaction in reflection and comfort in a slower, calmer life.

Studies of the human brain have revealed three significant physiological differences between introverts and extroverts. First, introverts have naturally busier, more active brains than extroverts. Though introverts look calm on the surface, our brains are bubbling with activity, and thus we require less external stimulation than extroverts. Too much external stimulation, in fact, leads to a feeling of overwhelm. Second, blood flows in different paths in introverted and extroverted brains. Introverts have more blood flow, but it flows in a longer, slower path than in extroverted brains. The blood in introverted brains flows to sections that are focused on internal things like remembering, solving problems and planning.[9] On the other hand, the blood in extroverted brains goes to those parts that are used for the processing of sensory experiences, what's happening externally.

Third, introverted and extroverted brains have different chemical balances. The activities of our brains are catalyzed by neurotransmitters, which are chemical substances that transmit nerve impulses. Extroverts require greater amounts of dopamine, a central neurotransmitter in the sympathetic nervous system. It is produced when people are active and in motion. As psychologist and author Marti Olsen Laney writes, "extroverts feel good when they have places to go and people to see,"[10] probably because they are flush with dopamine. Dopamine takes a short path through the brain and, in stressful situations, produces an "act and react" response. It can be credited for extroverts' ability to think and speak quickly and to thrive under pressure. It also helps them access their short-term memory rapidly, so their data-processing circuit is shorter and faster.

Introverts, on the other hand, require less dopamine, and when our brains have too much, we can feel anxious or overwhelmed. Our brains rely more on another neurotransmitter, acetylcholine, a neurotransmitter of the parasympathetic nervous system, which conserves and restores energy, producing a "rest and repose" posture. It produces a pleasurable sensation in introverts when we are thinking and reflecting. Acetylcholine, however, cuts a longer path through the brain, which explains why introverts may have difficulty accessing words or memories quickly and why we may be slow to react in stressful situations. Introverts often prefer writing to speaking, because writing uses a different neurological pathway in the brain than speaking does. Additionally, the slower acetylcholine tributary may produce a posture of calmness in introverts and cause us to move more slowly than extroverts,[11] which may explain why we are often less expressive with our bodies.

I have come to see that this information is valuable in combating the common feeling among introverts that we are not as smart as others.[12] For me, this insecurity used to surface every time I saw a spy movie with my extroverted friends. Before we even exited the theater, my friends would be reviewing the movie, grappling with its plot twists and misdirection. They could summon memories of detailed scenes and conversations quickly and make connections that I couldn't see yet. I felt slow and dense. I assumed that mental quickness was a barometer of intelligence.

As I have come to understand the difference in introverted and extroverted brains, I have realized that it is not a matter of intelligence but of different mental processes. I would often miss details in the movie because I would be more attuned to my internal state than the events on the screen. I also didn't have the accelerated access to my short-term memory so, as we reviewed the movie, I couldn't remember scenes and plot twists as quickly, nor could I talk about it at the same rate. I needed time to process internally, which was hampered by the fast-talking environment around me. After I had time to process it and reflect on it, I came not only to understand the overall plot but often, would see intricacies and connections that my extroverted friends had missed. My clear, long-term memory enabled me to ruminate on the details of the movie after others had forgotten them.

ECHOES OF INTROVERSION IN THE BIBLE

The Bible does not directly address personality categories such as introversion or extroversion. In order to be good interpreters of Scripture, we need to attend to the original historical, cultural and literary contexts that it was written in and for. I am hesitant to superimpose a psychological grid onto the Bible, which would have been completely foreign to the original writers and readers, so what follows are only suggestions or hints at the personality features that echo in the stories of biblical figures.

Jesus' closest disciple and the gospel mission's first apostle, Peter, stands out as a man with highly extroverted tendencies. Peter was upfront and aggressive, quick to speak and quick to act. He planted himself at the center of the group of disciples, bluntly spoke his mind and learned by making mistakes. He was the first to confess Jesus as the Messiah, and he was also quick to rebuke Jesus when Jesus said that his own messianic journey would go the way of the cross. Showing a tendency to act before thinking, Peter climbed out of the boat to meet Jesus in the waves, and then reconsidered and sank. He was courageous enough to stand up on the day of Pentecost and preach the gospel to thousands of Jews, seemingly without having previously reflected on his message! Peter was bold and active, taking center stage in the gospel mission. I have wondered whether the Gospel of Mark—which is traditionally attributed to a writer who accompanied Peter and recorded what he said about Jesus—is as action packed as it is because of Peter's extroverted influence. Mark's story flows quickly, punctuated by sharp narrative introductions and sudden entrances of new characters.

On the other side, there are several biblical characters that show signs of introversion. Jacob, patriarch of the nation of Israel, was described as a "quiet man" (Gen 25:27). Moses, when he was alone in the wilderness and encountered the God of his ancestors, he resisted God's call by saying he was "slow of speech" (Ex 4:10) and wary of the spotlight. Mary, the mother of Jesus, showed a reflective, introspective side as she "treasured all these things in her heart" (Lk 2:51). Another Mary, Martha's sister, chose to sit at Jesus' feet and listen to him when he dined in their home (Lk 10:38-42). Then there was Timothy, whom the apostle Paul felt the need to remind that the Holy Spirit is one of power and not of timidity (2 Tim 1:7), perhaps because Timothy let an introverted cautiousness turn into fear and passivity.

And finally, there was Zacchaeus. We might strain our necks a bit to note that Luke's famous tax collector didn't utilize his short stature to maneuver his way through the crowds to be near Jesus, but instead he climbed a tree to observe (Lk 19:2-10). His first inclination was to consider Jesus from a distance, and he seemed content to let Jesus pass without interacting with him. Unlike more aggressive biblical characters, Zacchaeus waited for Jesus to initiate with him, rather than pushing his way through the crowd to touch or talk to Jesus.

Although we do not know enough about most biblical characters to say definitively what their personality types were, we can say without hesitation that God used, and uses, people of all different temperaments to carry out his mission to the world. God does not seek to conform them to a particular mold, but he works within their unique personalities and utilizes their individual gifts both to bless them and to bless others.

3

Finding Healing

"Let the guest come so that the host may be healed."

AFRICAN PROVERB

There are times when I've really struggled to come to grips with being introverted in a culture where extroversion is so prized," my friend Veronica told me. "I'd like to think that the work of God might be displayed through my introversion, and not in spite of it."

Veronica's words sharply and poignantly capture the complexity of life as an introvert, with both the pain of feeling adrift but also the hope that God's power will transcend our personality type without obliterating it. Like many of us, Veronica knows, on some level, that introversion is a part of God's creative purposes for her, but she struggles to find peace with her temperament and to live as an introvert in a world that doesn't always understand or accept her.

In an extroverted culture, introverts can become the silent screens onto which others project their insecurities. Others may regard our quietness as arrogance, or they may interpret our tendency to observe in social situations as condescension. Some consider us to be silently judging them or storing up material for criticizing them. Sometimes they will view us as angry or contemptuous. On a short mission trip I took to Latin America, my host families thought I was *enojado*—angry—because I kept a distance from what seemed to me to be unruly social interactions. But it's not only extroverts who get a negative read on introverts; I have even caught myself interpreting the silence of my fellow introverts in a critical light.

Living as an introvert in a society and a church that exalts extroversion takes its toll, and shame cuts deep into introverted psyches that are bent toward self-examination. Add into that the hurtful experiences we all have in relationships, and our self-doubts are confirmed, pushing us toward isolation. As I was working on this book, I interviewed a variety of introverts, each with unique perspectives and experiences, and there was a universal sentiment among them that, in order to thrive as an introvert, healing is needed. We seek healing both from the internal wounds of distorted self-understandings and feelings of inadequacy, and from the outward wounds of alienation from others and exclusion from our communities. We desire the freedom to be ourselves and to love others as ourselves.

THE WILDERNESS

In anticipation of a romantic introverted adventure of self-discovery, I went to see the 2007 movie *Into the Wild*—a true-story depiction of a young man who crosses the country and survives in the Alaskan wilderness. Instead, though, I found myself deeply disturbed by the story of a man who was running from his troubled past and rejecting the people who loved him, even his utterly devoted younger sister. He thought that true identity was found in separation from others, yet he discovered that isolation did not lead to life and peace but to loneliness and, quite literally, death. In the wilderness his wounds festered until they became fatal.

Introverts' wounds usually begin in childhood. Our families of origin convey to us messages about introversion, which set us on a path of either self-acceptance or self-criticism. Psychologist Marti Olsen Laney describes the psychological toll that negative messages can have on introverts: "Growing up constantly being compared to extroverts can be very damaging. Most introverted children grow up receiving the message overtly and covertly that something is wrong with them. They feel blamed—why can't they answer the question faster? And defamed—maybe they *aren't* that smart. Forty-nine of the fifty introverts I interviewed felt they had been reproached and maligned for being the way they were."[1]

Some of the introverts I interviewed confessed their tendency toward depression. Psychologist Laurie Helgoe says that introverts are more likely to seek mental health services than extroverts. We may be in particular danger for depression because we internalize our emotions, and we may also carry inside us the dysfunctions of our families in ways that extroverts don't.[2] Nagging feelings of shame, loneliness, fear and anger can eat away at us like parasites. One introvert I know said his internal perspective can spiral into an icy, bottomless loneliness. While extroverts commonly feel loneliness when others are *absent*, introverts can feel most lonely when others are *present*, because ours is the aching loneliness of not being known or understood.

Some of the most painful stories I heard were told by introverts who grew up in extroverted families. While growing up, Lara was misunderstood by her extremely extroverted mother, and she has four brothers and sisters who followed in their mom's extroverted footsteps. Her mother found great happiness in turning strangers into friends and in being acquainted with a wide variety of people, experiences and topics. While the rest of the family's favorite activities took place in the presence of a large circle of people, Lara enjoyed reading alone in her room or spending time with one or two of her closest friends. Lara's mother was disturbed by her daughter's "loner" behavior patterns, and she made it her personal mission to push Lara into a more "normal" lifestyle. Often her mother made remarks to her friends that Lara "must have been adopted," which was devastating to her. She believed the criticisms that she was abnormal and consequently had a very poor self-image. When she compared herself to her extroverted mother and siblings, she considered herself worthless, with little to contribute to others.

Mike, a former student of mine, traces his introverted wounds to experiences in elementary school. He was convinced as a child that he was stupid, because whenever his teachers would call on him to answer questions, he was unable to respond quickly. When he would hesitate, his teacher would assume he didn't know the answer, and as a result, he received poor marks for classroom participation and preparation. His parents even hired a tutor to catch him up to the rest of the class. But Mike's hesitation at unexpected questions did not indicate mental slowness; rather it pointed to an introverted tendency to think internally. He now says that, because of his self-doubt, he has obsessively devoted most of his life to convincing himself and others that he is intelligent and articulate. He overcompensates by working and reading fanatically, still fleeing from the deep-seated fear that he is stupid. Like many wounded introverts, Mike fears humiliation.

As Laney astutely observes in *The Introvert Advantage,* "Having limitations is not the problem. It is the meaning we give limitations that causes so much pain."[3] In the previous examples, the "limitations" my friends had were restricted social energy, fewer friendships and a need to process internally. In themselves, these are neutral personality features. But it was the way my friends and those closest to them *interpreted* these aspects of themselves that persuaded them they were stupid and worthless. Finding healing as an introvert will not entail freedom from these characteristics. Healing for us will involve a new way of interpreting our natural personality traits.

The process of healing is complicated by the various threads that make up the infinitely complex human personality. The challenge lies in distinguishing between the healthy components of our personalities, those that are natural and to be celebrated, and the coping mechanisms that are the symptoms of our wounds. We will need to differentiate between healthy and unhealthy in both our internal thoughts and feelings and our external behaviors. Which of our tendencies are intrinsic to our introversion and which of them are symptomatic of unhealthy ways of coping?

For example, the wife of a dying patient, named Kirk, recently lamented to me that, even after forty-five years of marriage, she felt that she hardly knew her husband. When I asked her why, she responded, "Because he is an introvert, and he keeps everything on the inside." As we continued to talk about him, however, it became clear that Kirk's introversion was only a small part of his reluctance to share his inner world with others. In his childhood, Kirk had learned that closing off from people was the only way to protect himself in an abusive environment. He built an impenetrable wall around himself just to survive. Unfortunately, he never sought the healing that he needed and kept everyone, even his wife, at a safe distance. Kirk's rigid boundaries shielded him from further pain, but they also prevented him from experiencing intimacy with others.

Introverts follow a social pattern of removing themselves from others, but when is that a healthy discipline and when is that cause for concern? It is natural for introverts to distance themselves from others to do the necessary work of internal processing, but too often we use that as an excuse for avoiding others, even when we have the social energy to engage. For me, in learning how to distinguish between these different tendencies to withdraw, I have found two connotations of the word *retreat* to be helpful.

Two kinds of retreats. We commonly use the word *retreat* to describe two different kinds of actions. The first usage comes from the battlefield. The defeated army "retreats" from the victorious army when they are overwhelmed by force and strategy. "Retreating" in this sense is negative, as we surrender to the superior power of others and escape from them out of fear of further loss. This is the unhealthy retreat of the introvert—withdrawal from others because of fear or intimidation—and it is not a proper feature of introversion; it is a symptom of shyness or social anxiety.

But there is a second way we use the word *retreat,* especially in churches. We take a retreat to a place removed from the fullness and preoccupation of our ordinary lives. We do this not out of surrender to some superior power but rather to gain strength for reentry into the world with greater perspective and peace. At retreats we gather in order to be refreshed with God's vision for our lives and with a sense of God's presence even in our most mundane activities. This is the proper version of the introverted retreat. Scattered and fragmented through interaction in the outer world, we retreat in order find wholeness so that we may reenter the world with renewed vitality.

The shyness cycle. Introversion and *shyness* are not synonymous. Introversion is a natural personality trait where we go inside ourselves to process our experiences. Shyness, on the other hand, is a condition marked by fear or extreme anxiety in social situations. It is common for introverts to struggle with shyness, because if social skills and confidence are earned through experience, then it's logical that introverts who run low on social energy and, consequently, have less experience would struggle with uncertainty and tentativeness. Our fears are compounded when we take a risk and are misunderstood or rejected, leading us into greater self-doubt and social anxiety. Our painful emotions lead us further into ourselves, and we often resist sharing our feelings with others. This completes the shyness cycle, as we hide from social situations, even becoming cynical of social interaction, and seal ourselves off in our internal worlds.

As our damaged psyches become our gauge for reality, we begin to lose our grasp on what is true and what is false. Our vision of both our inner worlds and the outer world becomes distorted. One of the delusions I was under for a long time was that, because I spent so much time looking at my inner world, I had the only accurate grasp on what was true about myself. And while we do often know what is true of us, we do not possess a foolproof gauge for self-evaluation. Even the healthiest of people struggle to measure the world and themselves with an accurate yardstick, as the power of sin infects everyone's mind as well as his or her actions. Paul describes humanity's spiraling descent into disarray in his letter to the Romans, "For though they knew God, they did not honor him as God or give thanks to him, but they became futile in their thinking, and their senseless minds were darkened. Claiming to be wise, they became fools" (Rom 1:21-22). In our fallenness, which is not yet fully redeemed, we have a blurred vision of reality that infects our self-understanding. We must seek healing then through God's renewal of our inner worlds and through the input of others who might see us more accurately than we see ourselves.

TOWARD HEALING

Introverted wounds bleed *in* our minds and hearts, and bleed *out* in our behaviors, actions and relationships. The healing program for introverts, therefore, must also move in two directions: in and out, deeper and wider. As we seek to embrace our God-given identity as introverts, we journey inward. We seek the freedom and peace of self-acceptance, and we learn to identify and appreciate the gifts God has given us. But we must also move in an outward direction, into the realms of action and relationships, which will further and confirm our healing.

Journeying inward. Most introverts will begin their journey toward healing in the inward movement. One introverted pastor said that her inward journey has been all about self-acceptance. She's had to learn that it's okay for her to talk less, to process silently and to spend less time with people. She's even conceded that it may take more work for introverts to accept themselves and assert themselves than it does for others, because of our culture's extroverted bias. If introverts cannot begin to accept themselves then there is little hope of progressing in the outward movement toward community and relationships with others.

So learning to embrace our introverted identity on the deepest levels is absolutely essential for us, and it will give us courage to take risks and be resilient when we meet inevitable obstacles and disappointments. Our churches may call us prematurely to the outward world of relationships and actions, but we must feel at home within ourselves if we are to be truly faithful to God and to go out and act with care and compassion for others.

Although there are a number of insightful books describing introversion and helping introverts find self-acceptance, this book departs from the majority of them in where I suggest we locate the source of healing. Most psychology books will say that healing begins with embracing the gifts we have as introverts and understanding that, though our attributes may differ from what our extroverted world treasures, we have deeply valuable things to contribute.

I do think introverts have significant gifts, but I do not think healing originates from understanding our gifts. I am convinced that true healing ultimately comes from the outside; it comes as an act of hospitality, as we respond to and welcome the indwelling presence of the Creator God who "formed my inward parts" (Ps 139:13). Our healing prescription begins not in exploring the nature of our introversion, as important as that is; our healing comes in probing the depths of God's nature and discovering the identity and purpose he gives us. Our heavenly Father knows us even more intimately than we know ourselves. He sees us with perfect clarity and is able to speak into those parts of ourselves that no one else can reach. Our hope is in his work of freeing us from the false ways we identify ourselves and conforming us to the nature of his Son. We cannot find freedom in our introversion until we embrace our primary identities as sons and daughters of God.

Herein lies the deep irony in a Christian view of healing for introverts: as followers of Jesus, even introverted ones, our ultimate identity is never found in aloneness, but it is found in relationship to another. Our individualistic culture encourages us to find our identity in defining ourselves apart from others: who we are is how we differ from other people. But for Christians, personal identity is relational. We define ourselves in relationship to Christ: who we are is how we relate to him. The Son, sent by the Father, lives in us through the Holy Spirit, and we can't truly meet ourselves until we meet him.

There is a relatively unheralded but powerful story in Luke's Gospel; in it, an anonymous woman meets the One who has the true power to heal. Following his regular practice, Jesus is in the synagogue teaching on the sabbath. The teacher would sit while everyone else in the synagogue stood to listen, and all eyes would be trained on Jesus as he expounds the Scriptures. But an unexpected character enters: a woman who has been debilitated by a bent back for eighteen years. Luke depicts her as "bent over and . . . quite unable to stand up straight" (Lk 13:11).

Just a few verses earlier, Jesus had refuted the prevailing understanding that the guilty suffer while the righteous prosper, and now we encounter a flesh-and-blood illustration of a person who is suffering. Not only is this woman in excruciating physical pain, but her distress is compounded by the scorn she faces, social and religious exclusion. I picture her at the periphery of the scene in the synagogue, her back forcing her gaze to the ground. It is an outward manifestation of the shame and rejection she likely feels. She is invisible, overlooked by the religious people who want to protect their own righteousness by not associating with her. Their laws, heaped on top of the written laws of God, are meant to ensure that Torah is observed, but they also guarantee that outsiders stay on the outside. The law of sabbath rest was guarded with particular scrutiny; if Jesus were to heal this hurting woman on the sabbath it would violate the command to cease all work on the holy day.

One part of this story always stands out to me: "When Jesus saw her, he called her over." Seemingly just a prelude to the healing that is about to take place, I think these words indicate that profound healing is already occurring for this nameless woman. For eighteen years she has been less visible than all the "religious" people, less visible than their precious laws, even less visible than the animals they release to drink water on the sabbath but refuse her release on the same day. Yet Jesus sees her. She is not invisible to him. He doesn't move over to her at the side of the synagogue, but he calls her into the center of attention. He practices the biblical emphasis on welcoming the stranger, extending hospitality to an outsider. All those eyes that have overlooked her are now forced to focus on her. Before her body is healed, her heart is being restored, as she learns that God sees her, loves her and treasures her as his own.

For much of my childhood, I felt invisible, often lacking space to speak and relegated to the fringes of social settings, so this story speaks deeply to me. While introversion and a crippling disease in a shame-based culture may not share the same level of agony, the idea that God sees me and calls me to himself is healing for me. Other voices will try to categorize us and tell us what is wrong with us, but true identity is discovered as we meet the One who created us and as we allow him to identify us. We are never strangers or outsiders to Jesus.

For genuine inward healing to occur, this understanding of personal identity must move beyond the intellectual level that comes so easily to introverts and descend into the realm of the heart. It's the divide between the mind and the heart that leaves so many of us fragmented and incomplete.

In my late twenties, I was working as the young adults' pastor at a large suburban church, and I was also a chaplain at a nearby hospital. Part of my chaplaincy program involved participating in group therapy. Each week six chaplains and two supervisors would meet together in a highly intense setting to discuss the personal issues being unearthed during our visits with patients. To my surprise I began to see some disturbing patterns in my life and relationships that brought into question virtually everything I held to be true about myself. I was dismayed to discover how much of my ministry was motivated by a desire for approval and validation of my worth.

One evening I was taking a walk at a nearby lake, and I was praying aloud: "Lord, I don't really know who I am anymore and I don't really know what's going on. I really need to hear from you. Speak, Lord, and I will listen." Just a couple of seconds later, I heard a voice say "Hi!"

Startled, I looked around, attempting to make out another figure in the darkness. Walking along the short, stone wall to my left was a boy, about six years old. He was wearing a blue shirt, khaki shorts and flip flops, which was almost identical to what I was wearing (even stranger because it was cold outside, and I had been wishing I had put on something warmer before I left the house). He was also wearing headphones and walking along the wall in a contented, carefree manner. At first I thought he was alone and I wondered, *What mother would allow her child out in such an outfit in the cold?* But then I saw a young girl trailing about thirty feet behind him, also balancing along the wall. She walked past me without looking at me or saying anything.

After they passed, I stopped and stood there for at least five minutes trying to process what had just happened. I felt guided into the realization that the boy was me, dressed the same way, walking in the evening and "listening" (symbolized by the headphones), just like I was trying to listen. But there was someone there with him, who was silent and slightly distant . . . but still present. And then God spoke into the silence: "I know this is hard, but you are *not* alone." Through the disruptive, beautiful experience of God with me, walking with me, all the knowledge I had gained of his healing power began to take hold of my heart.

Journeying outward. Experts both in personality type and in Christian spirituality assert that the direction of growth is against our normal tendencies. While we may start being inwardly focused, we also have to move outward. Earle Page at the Center for Applications of Psychological Type observes that while introverts find primary vitality in reflection and contemplation, the overdevelopment of introversion can lead to "withholding, idiosyncrasy, or inappropriate intensity."[4] So even though I disagree with Freud's equation of introversion and narcissism, I do believe that introverts are susceptible to an unhealthy degree of self-preoccupation. In the language of emotional intelligence, we may have strong personal awareness but lack social awareness. We can become mired in our inner worlds, to the exclusion of relationships and actions that would bring the healing and joy we seek. Our inner reflections can become excessive to the point of inaction. Introversion should never be an excuse for laziness or sin. Understanding our introversion is not the end of our self-discovery and growth; it is a beginning point for learning how to love God and others as ourselves.

Thus the introverted trajectory of growth is toward relationships with others and relationship with the outside world. The love that is the ultimate goal of the Christian life cannot be restricted to inner stirrings, but it must be expressed in self-sacrificial action. Healing will come en route. We stretch as we take risks and move beyond our comfort zones. As we relate to others who are different from us, we begin to be freed from the assumptions we have made about them. We reject temptations to settle into a victim mentality, and instead deal constructively with our feelings of pain and exclusion, taking responsibility for our attitudes and actions. We may even find we need to reconcile with extroverts whom we have disparaged or misinterpreted. We find wholeness as we engage in what have traditionally been called the "outward" disciplines, such as fellowship, celebration, service and confession to others. We bless the body of Christ when we express our gifts within community and when we love at personal costs to ourselves. Though we may start with receiving the welcome of Jesus ourselves, it is not enough; we must also welcome the stranger, the outsider, the misunderstood, the suffering: "Welcome one another, therefore, just as Christ has welcomed you, for the glory of God" (Rom 15:7).

In the process, we are not aiming to become extroverts; we still firmly remain introverts and have a preference toward solitude. Our goal, rather, is to stretch our personality preferences without distorting them. We learn how to look outward but, at the same time, without losing our center.

In this book project, I had to resist my introverted temptation to spend all my time in my study reading, researching and writing, because it was the conversations and interviews I had with others that proved the most illuminating. The discovery of the most profound insight on my own did not compare to the exhilaration of truth stumbled on together. One conversation with another introvert brought more sparks of thought than a weekend at my desk. As I discussed my ideas with others and put words to my reflections, I found clarity that was lacking in my inner processes. I built bonds with others through our mutual experiences as introverts trying to live in Christian community. Introverted friends helped me to realize I was not only giving voice to my own thoughts about this topic; I was advocating for a community of introverted Christians who share frustrations and hopes for their lives and for the church.

Community is indispensable for our healing. We are strengthened as we give others authority to enter and speak into our lives. As Dietrich Bonhoeffer wrote in his classic book on community, *Life Together*, "God has willed that we should seek and find His living Word in the witness of a brother, in the mouth of man. Therefore the Christian needs another Christian who speaks God's Word to him. He needs him again and again when he becomes uncertain and discouraged, for by himself he cannot help himself without belying the truth."[5]

One particularly insidious behavior in introverts is the tendency to suffer alone. We internalize our dark emotions, often increasing our loneliness and closing ourselves to the love and insight that can bring healing and new perspectives. For my introverted friend Emily, the most profound thing she has learned to say to others is "I'm not okay." Others are able to mediate the gentleness of Christ to us when we are not able to be gentle with ourselves. God surrounded me with a chorus of gentle, introverted voices as I sought to embrace my own introversion—a spiritual director who saw God's handiwork, a therapist who helped me unravel the threads of my personality, a pastor who empathized with my ministry exhaustion and a supervisor who gave me permission to be an introvert in an extroverted profession. They met my self-denunciation with words and acts of affirmation and compassion.

Likewise, the extroverts in my life have significantly contributed to my healing. Some of my most affirming moments have been when extroverts have pointed out what gifts I bring to a group setting, or when they have expressed appreciation for the different perspectives I offer. They have convinced me that I have valuable things to contribute to others. Extroverts who have learned how to gently draw out the opinions of introverts and who give us the space to think quietly are truly God's grace to us.

I'll never forget a comment that Claudia, an introverted college student, said in a seminar at a summer conference. She had been profoundly shy and reticent during her first year of college. She kept to herself, and prying more than a few mumbled words out of her was an incredible accomplishment. She later confessed that she compulsively reviewed all her social interactions—what she said, what she did, how others reacted to her, what she should have said or done differently—out of desperation to find acceptance. But Claudia had a strong faith, and for the next four years, she committed herself to the community. She unwaveringly participated in small groups and Bible studies, and slowly gave others permission to enter into her life and to know her. She began to take longer forays out of her inner world and into community activities. She joined a group that ate lunch with homeless people on Sunday afternoons. An extroverted leader helped her identify her gifts and taught her how to use them for the sake of the community.

As Claudia's senior year drew to a close, she participated in a seminar I taught on the book of Genesis. We were discussing the idea of how being human, created in the image of God, means in part that we are created to be in relationship with one another. Claudia began to smile as she said, "I remember four years ago at this conference I had absolutely no one to talk to. I would go an entire day and say hardly anything at all. Now it's my last year, and earlier I walked into the cafeteria and I thought, 'Who should I talk to first?' "

Our outward journey of healing will usually progress in small steps. Most of our quality fellowship will be done in the context of one-on-one interactions or small groups. When we serve, we may choose roles that are behind the scenes. In social events, we may stand close to the door. Yet as we persevere, we will find that we are able to become more confident in and enjoy varieties of social situations. Though we can't change the directional flow of our energy—nor do we want to—we can build greater stamina in social situations so that we lose energy a little more slowly. We will begin to claim our introverted voices in an extroverted culture. And though our growth will move us into less familiar territories of relating to others, into speaking our minds and into engaging in external pursuits, we know that we will still return to solitude in order to complete our journeys.

THE LIMITATIONS OF PERSONALITY TYPE

As introverts who are followers of Jesus, we must remember that our introversion does not ultimately determine our thoughts and behaviors. Personality typing is a helpful way to understand ourselves and how to live authentically in the world, but it is not what centrally defines us. When we use our introversion as an excuse for not loving people sacrificially, we are not acting as introverts formed in the image of God. We who follow a crucified Messiah know that love will sometimes compel us to willingly choose things that make us uncomfortable, to surrender our rights for the blessing of others. We worship a God "who by the power at work within us is able to accomplish abundantly far more than all we can ask or imagine" (Eph 3:20). We must always be open to the sovereign God who can shake us to our cores, who gives us the strength to transcend the limitations of our humanness and to do things we never thought possible.

A story from the Gospels reminds us that we work out of an otherworldly power that supersedes the gifts and limitations of our personalities. Jesus sent out his disciples to proclaim God's kingdom and his power over unclean spirits, and he had insisted that they travel light, forbidding them to carry food, money or extra clothes. They were forced to rely on the hospitality and generosity of their hosts in a vulnerable and undoubtedly exhausting mission. Having completed this weighty task, they returned— tired, dirty and famished—only to find Jesus amidst a crowd clamoring for his attention. I can only imagine their disappointment and resentment when they spotted yet another hungry, needy, noisy crowd.

But when Jesus saw the disciples, he uttered the line that brings delight to the heart of every introvert, the invitation that I hope will usher me into the gates of heaven: "Come away to a deserted place all by yourselves and rest a while" (Mk 6:31). At last! It was time to find some seclusion, to rest, to celebrate, to make sense of all that had gone on, and to prepare for what was coming.

They boarded a boat and navigated toward their emancipation. Meanwhile, the crowds got wind of where they were going and rushed by foot around the lake to greet them on the other side! I can picture the scene as the disciples look up and see the lonely shore starting to fill with bodies. First a straggler or two, no big deal. Then a family, then another and, before long, an entire town. The introverts among the twelve must have groaned in despair. *Is there no relief?* But Jesus disembarked and received the crowd with love, teaching them well into the evening. As it grew late, the disciples tried one last strategy: "Jesus, it's dark, and after all, we are in a deserted place and everyone is hungry. Why don't you show some mercy on them and send them away to get some food?" The disciples were spent; they had nothing left to give. They had closed their hearts for the day.

To their puzzlement and dismay, Jesus responded "*You* give them something to eat" (Mk 6:37, emphasis added). The hunger of the crowds mirrored the emotional emptiness of the disciples, but Jesus knew about another source of life: a hidden metabolic process, one that is greater than food and more energizing than seclusion. But Jesus didn't just produce food out of the air, he sent the disciples into the crowds for food, forcing them to go out among the people they were trying to avoid. They wanted to withdraw, but Jesus wanted to reopen their hearts to the needs of others.

And then, out of the meager food they supplied, Jesus produced an extravagant banquet, enough for all with twelve baskets of leftovers. Even when our resources are at their lowest point, even when we have nothing to offer, we work out of a power that can take our scant reserves and overwhelm people with a mercy that heals both body and soul.[6]

4

Introverted Spirituality

"The healthy Christian is not necessarily the extrovert, ebullient Christian,
but the Christian who has a sense of God's presence stamped deep on his soul,
who trembles at God's word, who lets it dwell in him richly by constant
meditation upon it, and who tests and reforms his life daily in response to it."

J. I. PACKER, *A QUEST FOR GODLINESS: THE PURITAN VISION OF THE CHRISTIAN LIFE*

"Without knowledge of self there is no knowledge of God.
Without knowledge of God there is no knowledge of self."

JOHN CALVIN, *THE INSTITUTES OF THE CHRISTIAN RELIGION*

There is an ancient and beautiful monastic practice called "The Grand Silence." For centuries, at the conclusion of the evening prayers, monasteries have prescribed the cessation of speech, to be observed in all circumstances except dire emergency. This silence endures through the night until the first prayers the next morning, when as the sun introduces the new day, the quiet is broken by the reading or singing of Scripture.

I first encountered this tradition on retreat with several of my ministry partners while I worked as a college pastor. For many of them, a fervent group of extroverts, this period of silence was far from "grand." They squirmed through the evening, steadily growing more somber and weary. Though they acknowledged the value of the practice, the silence was a slow leak on their souls, sapping their vitality and energy for community.

For me, the lone introvert, not even the most haunting chants of the Psalms that resonated through the chapel at daybreak could compare to the transcendence of the Grand Silence. Monasteries may be homes of discipline and asceticism, but each night their members feast on a gluttonous banquet of quiet. I anticipated and relished those hours, often going deep into the night to savor the stillness. For a few glorious moments, I entertained the idea of making my cell my permanent residence.

In the fifth century, Saint Benedict, father of the monastic way, instructed his pupils to keep regular silence: "Therefore, because of the importance of silence, let permission to speak be seldom given to perfect disciples even for good and holy and edifying discourse."[1] Benedict understood that the first roles of the disciple are to listen and learn. Words, rather than issuing from a well of reverence and wisdom, often betray ignorance and immaturity.

Today Benedict's exhortation to keep regular silence seems like an idea from another dimension, eccentric advice from an antiquated culture. The ears of our culture pound with words, polluting our audioscape with constant white noise. It often feels like our world is locked in a prison of words. Henri Nouwen did not exaggerate when he declared "Over the last few decades we have been inundated by a torrent of words. . . . Words, words, words! They form the floor, the walls, and the ceiling of our existence."[2]

Probing further, Nouwen laments that in such a culture, "who can maintain respect for words? All this is to suggest that words, my own included, have lost their creative power."[3] He penned those thoughts before the advent of the cell phone, a device that has carved channels of verbosity into our airwaves, so that satellite-powered words now bounce around the cosmos. As the speed of our words has increased, so has the pace of our culture as a whole. People scurry from one task to the next. Visual and audio stimuli of all kinds race around us. Moving images, graphics, colors and noise have become part of the very atmosphere in which we live and breathe. In fact, recent studies are showing that our technologies are actually remapping the circuitries of our brains, so that concentration for long periods of time is becoming more difficult. Many of us can relate to this author's lament in *The Atlantic:*

> Immersing myself in a book or lengthy article used to be easy. My mind would get caught up in the narrative or the turns of the argument, and I'd spend hours strolling through long stretches of prose. That's rarely the case anymore. Now my concentration often starts to drift after two or three pages. I get fidgety, lose the thread, begin looking for something else to do. I feel as if I'm always dragging my wayward brain back to the text. The deep reading that used to come naturally for me has become a struggle.[4]

Ours is an overstimulated culture, and an insidious side effect is that our inner worlds are atrophying. As our world becomes more and more driven by external stimulation and our lifestyles mirror the dizzying speed of our technology, we focus outward at the expense of the inward. We take leaps and bounds in one direction but drift from another, which can have the effect of alienating us from ourselves, others and God.

My wife and I recently witnessed the disorienting nature of technology at a local movie theater. The next day, perhaps ironically, I recorded my reflections on my blog:

> There were three people in the rows in front of us who had their cell phones open during the entire movie. They were

text messaging and surfing the Internet and otherwise an-
noying people. As I saw those cell phone screens open during the movie, I observed that the people using them were
not fully committed to being anywhere during those two
hours. They were physically sitting in the theater, even sitting with others who accompanied them, but their minds
and hearts were scattered all over the place. They were not
fully present, in terms of their attention, to the visual and
auditory experience in front of them, they were not fully
present to their friends and family that they were sitting next
to, and they were not geographically present to the people
they were text messaging. They had a hand and foot in several different places that were disconnected, leaving them as
some sort of radical amputees. They were everywhere and
they were nowhere.

Aside from how piercingly bright a cell phone screen can
be in a dark movie theater and how bizarre it is to text message during an intense and complex spy movie, I got to
thinking about how handheld technology affects our sense
of personal identity. So many people walk through their lives
as ghosts, not fully present to anything, gliding through
places and around people but not really seeing or experiencing or being seen or experienced.[5]

In an increasingly fragmented, fast-paced, chatter-filled world,
I consider the greatest gift introverts bring to the world and the
church to be *a longing for depth*. Spiritually mature introverts offer
an alternative to our contemporary lifestyle, one that is thoughtful, imaginative and slower. For introverts, the quality of our
Christian lives is predicated on the quality of our inner lives. Introverts who flourish spiritually have descended deep into our
own souls and deep into the heart of God. My conversations with
spiritually minded introverts continually turned to the topic of

contemplative spirituality, with many describing themselves as "contemplatives."

CONTEMPLATIVE SPIRITUALITY

Contemplatives are most commonly associated with movements of people who shelter themselves off in monasteries in order to devote themselves wholly to prayer and reflection. But in many wings of the church today, contemplative spirituality is less of a specific community and more of a spiritual bent to which people in different traditions, from Catholicism to evangelicalism, subscribe. Sometimes referred to as mysticism, this spiritual mindset seeks to discover the presence of God in every aspect of human life. Contemplation appeals to people of many different temperaments, who find that their hearts cry out for a focus and a depth that modern life does not offer.

Introverts are often drawn to such spirituality, as it involves a quieter, more reflective lifestyle. On a basic level, to contemplate means to focus our attention on something, or in Christian spirituality, some*one*. The contemplative spirit is grounded in the conviction that God is communicating, through Scripture, through creation, through beauty, through our experiences, through our emotions and thoughts and bodies, through other people, and preeminently, through Jesus Christ. Another way of saying it is that the contemplative life embraces a spirituality of listening; God is speaking in manifold ways, and we aim to "listen" with all our senses.

At other times we seek to move beyond our senses. There is an ancient spiritual tradition, still a central practice in Eastern Orthodoxy, called apophatic spirituality. Also referred to as *via negativa* ("the negative way"), apophatic spirituality focuses on what cannot be grasped about God through rational thought, words or images. It emphasizes the hiddenness of God. This is in contrast to kataphatic or positive spirituality, which is focused on what *can* be known about God. Kataphatic spirituality is grounded in revelation—the words, images and other means through which God has chosen to disclose himself in the Scriptures, the created world and the incarnation of Jesus Christ. Evangelical theology and practice almost exclusively favors the latter form of spirituality.

Although we possess God's self-revelation in the Bible, God can never be encapsulated by words on a page or confined by precise doctrines. Words and tangible images are signs pointing to God, but they are not God himself. As useful and necessary as they are, they have a way of limiting or trying to control him. But as God revealed to the prophet Isaiah, "the heavens are higher than the earth, / so are my ways higher than your ways / and my thoughts than your thoughts" (Is 55:9). Contemplatives understand that God is a personal being whom we can relate to and experience, and if we wish to have a more profound experience of God, it's not a matter of trying to think thoughts higher than previously considered but a matter of sensing God on a different level that transcends words and rational thought.

Contemplatives value both forms of spirituality but understand that kataphatic theology can only take us to the threshold of mystery. Otto Kroeger and Roy Oswald explain that introverts are often attracted by apophatic prayer: "In this prayer form, we move in silence to quiet the mind and focus on a sacred word or phrase. Apophatic prayer tries to rid the mind of all images and forms so as to be open to encounter directly the Mysterious One. It is the desire of the meditator to listen to God, rather than talk to God."[6] As contemplatives quiet themselves to listen and simply rest in the presence of God, we learn that God is at once mysteriously sovereign and intimately present. God eludes our grasp and yet shows himself to be closer than we ever imagined.

Integration. Contemplation is also about integration, a way that we incorporate the divided fragments of our existence. Introverts in particular can feel that the world divides us from ourselves, that it takes from us. In contemplation we seek to draw together the divided fragments of our existence and present them to God who, in turn, finds us, restores us and draws the pieces together. Contemplatives seek God as the consistent thread in our disparate experiences, thoughts and circumstances.

While some might think that contemplatives are passive recluses who avoid contributing to the world, true contemplatives are deeply engaged in the world. Father Ronald Rolheiser says that "Contemplation is about waking up. To be contemplative is to experience an event fully, in all its aspects. Biblically this is expressed as coming 'face to face' with God, others, and the cosmos. We are in contemplation when we stand before reality and experience it without the limits created by narcissism, pragmatism, and excessive restlessness."[7] In true contemplation we practice being fully present—in mind, soul and body—to God and to ourselves. We seek to be fully alive to the subtle groaning of the Spirit and to the grace and wisdom being given in each moment.

Solitude. A feature of contemplation that appeals to introverts is solitude. We find permission for solitude from the example of Jesus, who at critical times in his ministry removed himself from his followers to pray. His ministry began not in a crowd but in the desert where, alone, he fought the temptations that Israel had succumbed to centuries earlier. In his solitude he confirmed his identity as the true Son of God, prepared to pursue the vocation God had given him.

Solitude is a way of creating space for the presence of Another, the voice of the One who called the world and us into existence. In a world filled with interminable chatter—others' and our own—God's voice is often muffled. Contemplatives know that God's voice rarely comes in thunder but rather in a whisper, creeping into the lives of shepherds in isolated settings or to prophets gasping in thin mountain air.

Contemplative solitude, though, differs from simple privacy. Privacy involves moving *away* from something, physically distancing ourselves from the draining world of outside stimulation.

Because activities and relationships are enervating for introverts, a constant and fundamental concern for us is energy level. We must diligently monitor our fuel gauge. Privacy is something all introverts require, and it has a way of naturally and psychologically restoring our energy levels.

Solitude, however, is as much of an internal state as it is a physical reality. In solitude we move *toward* something, toward an encounter with God that produces spiritual renewal. The Greek word for "energize" (*energeo*) appears frequently in the New Testament and often refers to the power of God in accomplishing great things beyond human abilities. Ephesians 1:20 says "God put this power to work [*energeo*] in Christ when he raised him from the dead and seated him at his right hand in the heavenly places." God's power is resurrection power, the very energy that triumphed over death in the person of Jesus and set the world ablaze with new creation. When we seek him in solitude we avail ourselves of resurrection power, finding restoration that supersedes any refreshment we can find in mere privacy.

Distance from distractions may form the context in which we find solitude, but it is not the goal. The goal of solitude is encounter with God, and the outworking of that encounter is transformation. Henri Nouwen, in his searching book on the spirituality of the Desert Fathers, *The Way of the Heart,* says that in solitude we experience both "the great struggle" against the compulsions of the false self and the "great encounter" with the loving God who offers himself as the substance of the new self.[8] In solitude we confront the forces that seek to shape us in their image and the alternative ways that we try to define ourselves, and we meet the God who offers us true identity and hear the voice that truly defines us and shapes us according to his image.

The spiritual life for introverts is bracketed by periods of solitude. We go there to gain God's eyesight for others and to receive his resources to engage in relationships and act in the world. And then, after we have responded to his call to work and to love, our spiritual lives culminate in solitude as we process and pray through the events of the day. Yet even for introverts, solitude is not entirely natural. Restlessness and loneliness can infiltrate our attempts at solitude, so we learn that solitude is a discipline to be cultivated.

Cultivating solitude: The examen. I find that spiritual exercises aid my attempts to cultivate solitude. At the conclusion of the day I do the examen, first proposed by St. Ignatius, which has helped me discover God's movements and tie together the diverse threads of my daily life. In the examen, I ask the Holy Spirit to aid me in surveying the events of the day, and as I review, I pay particular attention to the (1) times I sensed the presence of God and (2) the things I feel grateful for. As I walk through my day, observing my victories and failures, acts of love and acts of sin, I ask *Where did I see God? Were there times God seemed absent?* I pay attention to motivations and feelings I had during the day. Then I close my time by directly interacting with God. I ask, *Are there occasions for praise and thanksgiving? Are there things I want to confess? Particular petitions I want to offer?* If there are unresolved feelings or issues that I would like to work through with God before I go to sleep, this is the right time—without going into extensive analysis.

What I like about this exercise is that it allows for the internal processing that introverts require. As I have come to embrace my introversion, I have learned that my brain will process my day one way or another. If I do not do it before bed, then I will often lie awake while my brain races through the day or else my subconscious will attempt to do the work—with strange results—while I sleep. The examen gives a concrete, compact structure to my processing.

I also appreciate that the examen allows for a time of focused prayer. Introverts have a constant internal monologue rushing through our heads. In my case, I could just as easily call it a dialogue because I often talk out loud to myself! There is a very animated committee in my head that produces all kinds of imaginary scenarios, has fierce verbal jousts, and wrestles with any number of personal and world dilemmas, so the challenge has been allowing God into my internal conversations. My internal chatter is so constant that it becomes difficult for me to discern the voice of God. My spiritual director encouraged me, then, to pause and invite God into those conversations. It's not that I need to silence the conversation that comes so natural to me; it's that I need to allow God to assume his place at the head of the table. This advice squares with the wisdom of the examen, which invokes the Holy Spirit to guide our reflections on the day that has happened. The examen trusts that God works in conjunction with our minds to reveal his movement in our lives.

Working in solitude: Paying attention. Another related discipline I have learned from my spiritual director is the discipline of paying attention. I have met many introverts who say, "I need to get out of my head," but in many cases I give them the opposite advice: go deeper into your head! While we must be wary of self-preoccupation, I am convinced that we embrace our introverted gifts by listening to what is happening in our inner worlds. As I search my heart, I pray that it would not ultimately be me doing the searching but God—the Creator who knows me even more intimately than I know myself and who speaks to places of my soul that no other voice can reach. The Psalmist asks the Lord to "Search me, O God, and know my heart; / test me and know my thoughts" (Ps 139:23).

It may be that introverts are more equipped to hear and see what God is doing inside of them, while extroverts are more sensitive to his revelation in the outer world. God's speech to introverts may come in the form of inward thoughts or impulses, ideas that spring out at us, or words, images or feelings that surprise us or cut against the grain of our natural tendencies. My friend Casey says that in her introverted processing, she shifts back and forth from inner monologue to dialogue with God. She has occasional moments in which a thought will pounce in from an unknown source, and then she knows that God has joined the conversation in her head. As introverts, we need to take the activities of our inner worlds seriously in order to hear the overtures of God sounding in our lives.

In my experiences in Christian communities, I have frequently encountered a resistance toward this sort of "paying attention." Likely stemming from Jesus' radicalizing the Jewish law in his Sermon on the Mount, many Christians are suspicious of their own desires and inclinations. They are constantly scanning for such vices as lust and covetousness, and when they find them they seek to "cut [them] off" (Mt 5:30) or, in their interpretation, by power of will, push those sins down. A suspicion of our natural inclinations may indicate a healthy resistance to sin, but if our version of "cutting off" sin means that we ignore the deeper messages that our longings send us, then we are dealing with distorted desires ineffectively. And it can stunt the growth of introverted believers who are predominantly oriented toward their inner worlds.

I was part of two men's accountability groups in college, and we dedicated hour after hour to confessing our troubling desires and having others pray that we would stop having them. What we didn't do is look at our desires more carefully, and try to discover what was underneath them. If negative desires—such as lust or comparison—are distortions of good, holy desires, then what is it that we are truly hoping or longing for? Our negative desires are windows into what we truly want. How can we listen to the good desires that underlie the negative ones, so that we can act on those good desires? How can we pray that God will begin to fulfill those desires that he's implanted in us? To curtly dismiss our disturbing desires is usually to only give them greater power; by listening to them and asking questions of them, we give power to what is underneath.

Introverts can, naturally, lead the way in listening to the subtle workings of our hearts, and as we spiritually mature, teach others how to distinguish between what is genuine and what is false.

EMBRACING OUR RHYTHMS

A proper understanding of Christian spirituality will embrace the entire person, not simply the person's "spirit." If the preeminent commandment is that you should "love the Lord your God with all your heart and with all your soul and with all your mind and with all your strength" (Mk 12:30 NIV), then our theology and practice of spirituality must address each aspect of our humanness. An introverted spirituality must take into account our *rhythms*, the dynamic interplay between our bodies, souls, minds and emotions. We must learn to "listen" to *each* part of our nature if we are to find balance and peace in our introversion.

Larger rhythms. A larger rhythm, universal for introverts, is the movement of engaging the world in a reflection-action-reflection pattern. This rhythm echoes some of our faith's foundational stories. In Genesis 1, before God begins his creative work, his Spirit hovers over the waters, seeming to scan the amorphous mass, poised and preparing to act. Then throughout the chapter there is a clear repetition of God creating and then reflecting on what he has made. Day by day of the creation week God not only acts but pauses and appraises what he has done. Most days, in fact, are not complete until God has looked on his work and assessed it as "good" (Gen 1:4, 10, 12, 18, 21, 25, 31). God's reflections separate the actions from one another and establish an order in the world that contrasts with the shapeless blob of watery chaos of the opening verses (Gen 1:1-2). At the conclusion of the six days of creation, God evaluates his the creation of humans as "very good" (Gen 1:31) and sets aside an entire day for restful reflection on his completed work. The sabbath day is not an afterthought, a day tacked on at the end, a mere poetic gesture. The sabbath is the consummation of the creation week, the celebration that the world has been created by and for God, and that order has triumphed over chaos. We reserve a day to rest and reflect on that reality and to free others to do the same.

God has imprinted seasons of work and reflection into the world he created, and he models for us both daily and weekly rhythms of reflection. Habits of reflection help us to find meaning and patterns in our lives and to battle against the chaos. There is a tendency for our actions and days to flow into each other and to mesh in a way that exerts control over us, but disciplines such as the examen allow us to reflect with God on his movements in our daily lives. Sabbath rest enables us to see broader patterns of the Spirit's work and teaches us not to capitulate to the restless activity of our culture. Sabbath gives us permission to do what out introverted hearts cry out for: to restfully reflect, contemplate, observe, retreat into and marvel at God's creation.

Smaller rhythms. As I have gotten older, I have learned to pay attention to my rhythms and to understand that when one part of my routine suffers, all of me suffers. I spent one summer in college, at the age of twenty-one, in a complete daze. I was on a short-term missionary team trekking through southern Mexico, visiting Christian communities at several universities. Two weeks in, I reached a level of fatigue that would endure throughout the remainder of the summer. I attributed it to the humidity, a poor diet, or my unfamiliarity with the language and customs. I resolved that I could never be a missionary, because I just didn't have the physical and emotional constitution to thrive. It wasn't until recently that I realized that my overall fatigue was a result of my introversion. Being on a missionary team, staying together in cramped quarters, and interacting with a very extroverted subset of Mexican culture left me exhausted and even resentful. It wasn't that I should be excluded from missions for the rest of my life, it was simply that I needed to find space to refuel.

My spiritual director, also an introvert, once remarked that it's incredibly important for him to get eight or nine hours of sleep a night in order to function. Many of the other introverts I interviewed agreed that they required more sleep than average. Introverts need to not only refuel mentally but physically as well. It's important that we pay attention to the mundane as well as the sublime, as it's the mundane that makes the sublime possible.

A rhythm that I have observed in myself is the importance of placing solitude somewhere near the beginning and end of my day. If I rush out the door in the morning, I feel disoriented and frustrated through much of the morning. And if I spend all evening with people, then I have a hard time sleeping at night. I have learned to get up earlier in the morning to read and pray, and I am consistent in taking a solitary walk in the evening to process through the events of the day. These rhythms have enabled me not only to find more peace within myself but also to be more present to others when they are looking for my support.

AN INTROVERTED RULE OF LIFE

A rule of life is an ancient practice; it is a way of structuring life in order to bring every aspect under God's gracious authority and to increase our awareness that all of life is permeated by God's presence. The rule can be communal, as in the case of St. Benedict's honored rule, or personal. It involves repeated activities and relationships that are tailored toward an individual's unique makeup and rhythms. A proper rule of life applies not only to the spiritual or devotional life, but also to work, relationships, physical habits and other facets of life. The rule of life counters our tendency to partition off the spiritual dimension from the rest of our lives.

I want to propose an introverted rule of life. While people of all personality bents will find a rule helpful, introverts in particular can benefit from the order and discipline it offers. Given the frenetic speed and activity of our world, we need to order our lives in such a way to maximize our social energy and to carve out several places for solitude. The rule of life works with the internal and external rhythms we discover as we come to embrace who we are. This is not simply a schedule or a calendar; a rule of life opens us to the awareness of God's presence, not only in our moments of quiet but in all aspects of our lives.

My variation on the standard rule of life revolves around our rhythms of energy and aims at finding a structure that enables us to receive God's power. I propose the following questions for helping other introverts discover their own rules of life:

1. What are the times of the day when I feel the most energized?

2. When do I feel the most tired?

3. How much sleep do I need?

4. What are the physical habits that energize me? drain me?

5. When do I most feel the need for solitude?

6. How do I find soul rest?

7. What are the spiritual disciplines where I feel most restored by God?

8. What are the relationships in which I feel the most refreshed? most drained?

With these questions, introverts can begin to establish the rhythms that bring harmony to their minds, souls, bodies and relationships. We can establish disciplines and patterns that we practice daily, as well as those that we practice weekly, monthly or yearly. By way of example, when I am in full-time ministry, an average weekday for me involves these disciplines:

- Morning devotions and writing
- Several short breaks of solitude throughout the workday
- Afternoon reading and silence

- Time with my wife or friends in the evening
- Late evening walk and practice of the examen
- Seven or eight hours of sleep

These are the daily rhythms that accord with my own unique makeup. I have found that structuring my day in this way enables me to maximize my relational energy, which fades during the day. Given the social and spiritual demands of ministry, I require two or three spaces for extended solitude as well as niches of solitude throughout the day. This is both for my own emotional health and for the benefit of those I pastor. After work I take a time of solitude, in order to bracket my workday and to be present to my wife for her extroverted processing when she comes home. My evening walk brings closure to my day and to the larger pattern of solitude-action-solitude that my days assume. The seven or eight hours of sleep a night, as well as regular exercise, ensure that I feel restored in the morning. I also practice broader rhythms, such as a weekly sabbath, monthly meetings with my spiritual director and two annual personal retreats.[9]

Other introverts, perhaps those who do not have such social requirements in their jobs, may not require as much solitude on a regular basis, though others may require more. For some, solitude needs to come in one large chunk of time, for others, solitude is best scattered throughout the day. Each person's rule will be unique. The rule of life, if practiced properly, should be liberating, not constricting. We will have to balance order with flexibility—acknowledging that life, and God, cannot be simply categorized or controlled.

The reality is *not* that we lack structure in our lives and we need to install it; rather, we *already have* rules of life, whether acknowledged or not. We navigate our days in certain ways, with habitual practices and disciplines. The conscious practice of a rule of life enables us to institute healthy and dependable rhythms that enable us to love God and others as ourselves. Following are more suggestions for disciplines to incorporate into your rule of life.

Intercession. For centuries, monasteries have been centers of ongoing intercession for the world. Monks do not cloister themselves off with the intent of escaping the world, but rather they consider their communities to be places where they can engage the world through their shared vocation. As they sing the Psalms throughout the liturgical hours, they sing on behalf of victims of poverty, injustice and oppression, and they sing for peace and reconciliation between the nations. Likewise, introverts in solitude can engage the world through interceding on behalf of others. If we practice solitude properly, we grow in compassion and love for others. As we are present to God, we are present to God's world. Intercession is a vehicle for ushering his kingdom and its righteousness into a world mired in darkness. If we practice solitude properly, we grow in compassion and love for others. As we are present to God, we are present to God's world.

Study and reflective reading. By virtue of our need for privacy, introverts tend to read more than extroverts. Study, therefore, is a natural discipline for us. What we read will be tailored to our particular interests. Theological study can be done in a way that is not merely academic. Slow, contemplative readings of longer portions of Scripture enable us to hear larger themes, both in Scripture and in our own lives. One friend said that she found the Gospel of John to be particularly appealing to her introverted side, as John moves slower than the other Gospels and probes deeply into ideas and the relationship between Father and Son. We can also practice private or communal *lectio divina* ("divine reading"), in which we savor each word and listen for God's direct speech to us.

Journaling and writing. Journaling has been an important discipline for me because it puts concrete form to my internal conversation. Even though I process internally, recording my thoughts on paper brings further clarity and coherence. Occasionally, I will even write out my prayers—not only to ensure that I remain focused but also so I can review them and further appreciate God's answers. There is a mysterious, spiritual component to writing. We may start writing our words but then find that our words are being written for us. We may find we are in the midst of an encounter with God, writing things we did not intend, discovering things we did not see.

Silence and centering prayer. There are certain times when we need to quiet the internal conversations in order to fully attend to the movement of the Spirit in our lives. At times the conversations in our very active minds become deafening, and we're unable to sort one from another. Worse, we're unable to discern the voice of God. In periods of silence, which can be any length of time, we seek to clear out the noise that clutters our mind. The goal of silence is not necessarily to hear the profound word from God, but simply to spend time with our Father—in which God may or may not speak.

Centering prayer is a prayer style in which we still our minds, allowing any conscious thoughts to dissolve away. We allow ourselves to be caught up in the holy, as someone sitting at the shore is swept up in the immensity of the ocean. Sometimes it helps to repeat a word or short phrase in order to focus our minds, such as the Jesus prayer: "Lord Jesus Christ, Son of God, have mercy on me, a sinner."

Sabbath. Patterned after God's resting as the consummation of the creation week, the sabbath is not only a time of cessation from work but it is a time reserved for intentional reflection oriented toward God. Introverts benefit from regularly setting apart longer periods to gather up the fragments of their lives and thoughts, and to present them to God through prayer or journaling. To rest and reflect are countercultural activities in our world, and they enable us to step out of the hurried, relentless activity of our culture and to observe the larger direction of and patterns in our lives.

A FALSE DICHOTOMY

The regular practice of these and other disciplines prepare introverts to lovingly engage the world. Sometimes people make an artificial distinction between the contemplative tradition, or "introverted" spirituality, and the activist tradition, or the more "extroverted" spirituality. Jeanette Bakke, author of *Holy Invitations,* explains that, until recently

> many Christians viewed contemplation with a suspicious eye, due in part to popular Western culture, which places contemplation and action at two opposite ends of a continuum. Many considered contemplation to be a kind of passivity, perhaps even a kind of laziness. They assumed that people were waiting for God to do something rather than engaging in the challenges of life. But this is not how it has been lived out. It used to be common knowledge that people of prayer become people of action flowing out of their relationship with God.[10]

If we are sensitive to the movements of God in our lives, we will not only devote ourselves to lives of prayer but in Christian activist Shane Claiborne's words, we will seek to "become the answers to our prayers" for the world.[11] In contemplation and solitude, we often find the impetus to act.

Kidnapped from his British home by a tribal Irish king, near the turn of the fifth century, Patrick endured six years of enslavement as a shepherd, tending sheep on Irish hillsides. In his aching loneliness, he rediscovered the Catholic faith of his parents, who were citizens in the British Isles that were governed by Rome. He dedicated himself to unceasing prayer, and one day he heard a distinct voice: "Your hungers are rewarded; you are going home. Look, your ship is ready." Patrick responded to the mysterious voice, trudging some 200 miles to the sea, where he met a group of sailors who granted his passage home. Years later, he heard another voice—this time an Irish multitude pleading with him "We beg you to come and walk among us once more." Patrick heeded that voice and became the apostle to Ireland, St. Patrick, the man universally considered as the one who brought Christianity to the island.[12]

Patrick's hours on Irish hillsides, braced by continuous prayer, attuned him to the voice of God. His six years of solitude prepared him to hear the call that would rescue him and then later summon him to a life of radical love, committed to rescuing the very people who had been his captors.

5

Introverted Community
and Relationships

"Let him who is not in community beware of being alone.

Into the community you were called, the call was not meant for you alone;

in the community of the called you bear your cross, you struggle, you pray.

You are not alone, even in death, and on the Last Day you will be only one

member of the great congregation of Jesus Christ. If you scorn the

fellowship of the brethren, you reject the call of Jesus Christ, and thus

your solitude can only be hurtful to you."

DIETRICH BONHOEFFER, *LIFE TOGETHER*

This is the chapter I didn't want to write. In my years of disciple-ship as an introvert, I have progressed in embracing my identity as a child of God and have cultivated a rich spirituality. I have developed leadership skills that are congruent with my introverted nature, and I have even taken strides in sharing the gospel as myself. But when the conversation turns to Christian community and relationships, I feel as an outsider looking in.

As I write about relationships, I draw more from theory than I do from experience. My failures in this arena have outnumbered my successes. Though I feel the universal human desire to know and be known, my knowing is more intellectual than emotional. So I have loaded this chapter with practical suggestions for getting involved in community, but I'm still trying to take them myself.

I'm someone who has received the accusation of living in the proverbial ivory tower as a borderline compliment. If I could, I would spend hours every day in my study—thinking, reading and writing—polishing the stones of my ivory tower to shimmering perfection. So much of me wants to be lost in my grand ideas and reflections, away from the noise and urgency of other people, but I cannot escape the fact that growth invariably involves the messiness of genuine human contact and the struggles of intimacy. I've yet to find a mature believer, either in this age or in the previous ages of the church, who says you can grow into the full stature of Christ without bumping up against brothers and sisters on a regular basis: "As iron sharpens iron, / so one person sharpens another" (Prov 27:17 TNIV).

THE GIVEN OF COMMUNITY

We have looked at dimensions of the Christian life with an introverted lens, dimensions that Scripture assumes take place in the context of shared community life. In biblical cultures, personal identity was intertwined with family and tribal associations, and people could not conceive of themselves outside their basic community affiliations. An individual was an extension and representative of his or her community.[1]

However, the individualistic nature of current Western culture tries to convince us that community is optional or peripheral. This individualism has bled into our evangelical theology and practice; we have often placed our focus on the relationship between individual persons and God at the expense of the communal emphasis that permeates the Old and New Testaments. Justification by faith, in our interpretation, has relevance for the particular sinner but has little bearing on our entrance into a community of faith. The evangelical phenomenon of the megachurch both satisfies our sense of duty to attend corporate worship and our ardent insistence to remain anonymous. We may be tempted to remain on the edge of a community, or to float from one community to the next, without making commitments or becoming known. If we stay on the outskirts we don't owe anyone anything and people don't expect anything. We avoid rejection but we deprive ourselves of intimacy and spiritual growth. It's in community that we learn how to love, how to serve, how to listen, how to forgive.

As someone who finds active participation in a community less than scintillating, I need to remind myself regularly of the biblical emphasis on community. In the opening pages of Scripture, we learn that to be made in the image of God is to be in relationship. God was determined to create humankind in *"our"* image (Gen 1:26), a phrase that hinted at the divine community that would be revealed as the story would unfold—Father, Son and Holy Spirit. Human communities reflect and are grounded in the trinitarian community. After the Fall of our first ancestors, humans bent toward division and distance, but God committed to reuniting a disintegrating world. The community of believers is the locus of God's saving activity. He forms us in communities of rescued individuals, whom he sets apart in covenant relationship with himself.

God's redemptive movement in history through community. God's first large move toward regathering a splintered world took shape in the call of Abraham and the threefold promise the Lord gave him. Each aspect of the promise related to community and was to be embraced in community: (1) *blessing,* so that the nations would be blessed through him (Gen 12:2); (2) *progeny,* as many sons and daughters as the stars in the sky (Gen 15:5); and (3) *land,* so that this immense family would have a place to dwell and thrive (Gen 15:18-21). The ultimate goal is that Abraham would not only be the father of Israel but the father of a worldwide community of faith, as the other nations would see the unity, abundance and faithfulness of Israel and be drawn to their God. God's plan of salvation is so much more comprehensive than individual sinners being rescued from the guilt of their particular transgressions.

God continued his work of restoring community in the ministry of Jesus of Nazareth, Abraham's descendant. Jesus re-formed the twelve tribes of Israel in calling twelve disciples, and he referred to his followers as brothers and sisters (Mt 12:50). At the Last Supper, he presided at the table as the head of the household, gathering his disciples around him as his family. In the new covenant community that formed after his death and resurrection, people entered into the community through the sacrament of baptism, which not only symbolized cleansing from the stain of sin but was an initiation rite into a new family. In the first-century church, to be a Christian was to be a member of the community. In the picture of the ancient church in Acts 2, we see that the first believers, even as their numbers swelled, lived as they were one single unit, and they invited others not only into belief but into their family.

The promises of God's redemption are to be embraced in the context of shared life where people are bonded together in love, with mutual obligations to one another. This intimacy stems from Jesus' prayer to the Father, the night before going to the cross:

> As you, Father, are in me and I am in you, may they also be in us, so that the world may believe that you have sent me. The glory that you have given me I have given them, so that they may be one, as we are one, I in them and you in me, that they may become completely one, so that the world may know that you have sent me and have loved them even as you have loved me. (Jn 17:21-23)

Similarly, the author of Hebrews maintained that community is an indispensable part of our lives as Christ-followers: "Consider how to provoke one another to love and good deeds, not neglecting to meet together, as is the habit of some, but encouraging one another, and all the more as you see the Day approaching" (Heb 10:24-25). The context in which this exhortation is found is just as striking: the Lord has written his laws on our hearts and will no longer remember our sins and lawless deeds (Heb 10:16-17); through the blood of Jesus, our new high priest, we have the right to enter with confidence into the presence of God, which was once sheltered by the temple curtain (Heb 10:19-22). These are beautiful, redemptive promises and the theological anchors of evangelical faith. Yet while the author of Hebrews envisaged a collected community of believers strengthening each other and reminding one another of these truths, the evangelical emphasis has been on the experience of the individual believer, relegating community participation to a secondary priority.

Finally, in the last act of the biblical story, we see a consummated age that does not have solitary, disconnected individuals living an ethereal existence but a worldwide community dwelling in a garden city, illuminated by the very presence of God. People of every nation will be drawn together across all dividing lines—Jew and Gentile, male and female, bound and free, introvert and extrovert—and will be gathered together at the throne of the Lamb who was slain.

PARTICIPATION AND BELONGING

The story of individualism and self-determination that our culture tells us cannot be reconciled with the biblical story of community and interconnected relationships.

Myths of belonging. Yet introverts may be in particular danger of falling captive to the individualistic assumptions of our culture, because in these assumptions, we can find intellectual justification for our bent away from the stress and exhaustion that we incur through interacting with others. We are often quick to embrace this message if only to avoid facing our fears of rejection and exclusion. Joseph Myers, in his book on community and small groups, *The Search to Belong,* exposes what he calls a common "myth of belonging": more personality=more belonging. "Many people believe that some have a natural ability to belong. They assume that if a person is more gregarious, more extroverted, he or she will have little trouble experiencing community, whereas those who are shy will struggle to belong."[2]

Behind this myth, though, lie more subtle and detrimental assumptions about the forms that healthy Christian community is supposed to take and what "faithful" participation looks like in these communities. It's easy to look at the ancient community in Acts 2 and conclude that the truly faithful community, the one where the face of God shines and the winds of the Spirit blow, is the one in which people are constantly together. Thus, it is a temptation for churches to define spiritual maturity as attendance: regular worship, participation in a committee or leadership team, and involvement in a small group. The implicit thought is that the mark of true, progressing discipleship is participation in an increasing number of activities. Along with attendance should come a steady increase in the number of people you know and who know you. Periodic worship attendance, hesitance to join many activities or a tendency to be elusive in social settings lands you squarely in the "uncommitted" camp.

Some churches also gauge a person's commitment by the amount of personal vulnerability shown. Many evangelical communities lay particular emphasis on "sharing." Our intimate relationship with God, available through Jesus Christ, ought to be mirrored by transparent, vulnerable, intimate relationships, so public testimony is encouraged. We can strengthen the faith of others, and grow in spiritual maturity ourselves, by laying bare the details of our personal lives. Henri Nouwen discussed the expectations in church culture about sharing: "We have been made to believe that feelings, emotions, and even the inner stirrings of our soul have to be shared with others. . . . In fact, people who prefer to keep to themselves and do not expose their interior life tend to create uneasiness and are often considered inhibited, asocial, or simply odd."[3] This practice can create uncomfortable intensity and can marginalize introverts who are hesitant to share their inner lives with more than a select few. Introverts have layered personalities, and they prefer to slowly unpeel the layers as they bond with people over time.

Sometimes introverts will resist sharing themselves because of bad experiences. Many introverts will relate to a scenario like the following. An introverted woman spends hours contemplating a thought or observing a pattern in her life. She turns it over in her mind until it becomes a companion to her and then decides to share it in the context of a small group. When she musters up the courage to voice it, trembling as she puts words to this precious inner stirring, someone in the group cuts her off when she pauses in the middle, her thought still building steam. This person quickly tells her that she shouldn't feel the way she does or else counters with a story of her own, which only tangentially relates to what the introvert was saying. Nouwen's words perfectly capture the sense of personal violation and emptiness: "Often we come home from a sharing session with a feeling that something precious has been taken away from us or that holy ground has been trodden upon."[4]

Because of these assumptions in many churches about what constitutes participation, we can become convinced that the faithful word in the Christian life is always *yes*. When we are asked to participate in an activity or group or sharing time, if we are really committed to community, if we truly trust God, we think we must answer "yes." Conversely, *no* is the unfaithful word. *No* is the word that shuts us out of community, that doesn't trust God and is closed to others and his work. Yet *no* is an indispensable word for introverts who need solitude and space to refuel and reflect. Without "no" we are unable to fully engage with others and to exercise our gifts in our communities. Saying "no" at times enables us to wholeheartedly say "yes" at other times. When we say "no" for good and important reasons, we are saying "yes" to the God who has formed us as introverts.

Belonging and personality. The measurements that churches use for determining the level of participation and commitment can fail to take into account different personality types. Myers notes that "we tend to validate only those ways in which we want people to participate. In truth, people participate in many ways."[5] Despite church's expectations, the introverted path in community may not conform to presuppositions churches have about involve-ment.

Myers claims that what determines belonging is not how a church defines it but whether an individual actually feels a sense of belonging to a community. He takes a subjective approach to belonging. People may feel an intimate sense of belonging through any degree of participation. A person can faithfully sit in the back pew of worship services, rarely talking to anyone and still feel a genuine connection to the community. I once overheard a conversation between two coworkers that illustrates that people can be deeply committed to a community even when appearances might indicate otherwise. The one coworker noted, "There are these two really introverted women at our church. They don't participate in many activities or talk all that much. They are the last people you would think would give much to the church, but the two of them are by far the most generous benefactors of our missions budget."

Similarly, someone can interact in a social setting without revealing much about herself yet still feel a lasting bond with that group. An introvert I know has worked behind the scenes in her church for eight years, and some in the community still don't recognize her, but she feels a passion for that community and where it is going. When weighing the decision to leave that church for a more active and influential church, she declined because of her sense of attachment to her church. Another introverted friend of mine said that he most appreciates church activities that involve shared action and few wasted words. His most satisfying community experience came as he participated in a men's group that painted and repaired houses for the shut-ins in their congregation. He found this kind of group easiest to enter, and he valued the relationships he had there, even though their conversations rarely wandered from tools and paint.

At the end of all this, what I found is that while most introverts acknowledge the indispensability of community, that does not mean that we endorse the models and standards of involvement that many churches prescribe. Too often churches ask introverts to change, rather than stretching their own understandings of participation.

The introverted spiral. As introverts seek to enter into and participate in particular communities, their trajectory of commitment may take a different shape than that of their extroverted counterparts. Extroverts, who want to increase their level of involvement, may proceed roughly in a straight line as they move from the periphery into the nucleus of the community. They move from stranger to acquaintance to participant to core member as they increase the breadth and depth of their relationships, finding more energy as they progress into the community. The journey of introverts into a community, however, is better conceptualized as a spiral. They take steps into a community, but then spiral out of it in order to regain energy, to reflect on their experiences and to determine if they are comfortable in that community. They move between entry, retreat and reentry, gradually moving deeper into the community on each loop.

The introverted path into community, much to the confusion of many extroverts, never reaches a point in which the spiraling form is shed. The spiraling shape persists even for introverts who are thoroughly committed to a community. Sometimes introverts feel the need to step outside of a community for a period of time, even after years of faithful participation. Other times introverts may continue to attend events but distance themselves emotionally and socially from all but their closest friends. These outward movements are often not an indication of spiritual atrophy or waning enthusiasm, but they are simply part of normal introverted patterns. In community, introverts follow a rhythm of *engage,* then *retreat.* Too much time in social interaction, no matter how satisfying, is disruptive and disorienting for introverts, and they need to step back to rediscover a sense of identity. They can lose themselves in community and need to retreat into solitude in order to be restored into shape and to find the power to give themselves fully to others when they reengage.

An introverted college student I worked with, Trevor, encountered several reactions when he chose to step outside of his community after two years of consistent participation. Extroverted leaders chided him for his lack of commitment and were convinced that his pulling back was indicative of a larger spiritual problem infecting his heart. The pastor of the community arranged meetings with him to understand what was happening and what was the source of his dissatisfaction with the group. These efforts, as well intentioned as they were, only pushed him further away instead of drawing him back into his previous level of commitment. But his introverted friends, he said, "were far more willing to ride it out with me." They listened and continued to interact with him as they always had, not judging his motives or actions. They understood his natural propensity for retreat from the high-paced energy and demands of the community. In giving him the permission to spiral in and out of community, they affirmed his journey and gave him the freedom to be an introvert.

GIFTS TO OFFER
People participate in community in different ways, and people

move among community at different rates. We all have our own pace, and there are times in our individual lives of faith when we move at different speeds. Sometimes our progress comes in leaps and bounds, but most of the time it feels slow. The point is not how fast we're moving, the point is that we are moving.

We also exercise our gifts in different ways in community. One of the strongest hopes that introverts articulated to me was a desire to make contributions to their communities. As introverts grow in understanding how to maneuver in community, we are greatly helped in knowing what we have to offer others, more fully discovering our gifts as we seek to use and cultivate them. Here are some gifts that introverts have to offer.

Compassion. Henri Nouwen asserted that "compassion is the fruit of solitude and the basis of all ministry." He discovered the paradox that "it is in solitude that this compassionate solidarity grows. In solitude we realize that nothing human is alien to us, that the roots of all conflict, war, injustice, cruelty, hatred, jealousy, and envy are deeply anchored in our own heart."[6] The further we probe into the depths of our hearts, and the good and the bad that lies within, the further we are able to enter into the inner worlds of others. Introverts, therefore, are capable of powerful compassion and are often very effective therapists and counselors.

My former colleague Cynthia, a pastor and hospice chaplain, is one of those introverts who seems to exude compassion from her pores. Anyone who spends a little time with her can see that she cares about people, especially about those that others are prone to overlook. Her compassionate presence has been transformative for her patients, whose greatest pain is often not physical but the spiritual and emotional pain of isolation. She is able to sit and empathize with her patients, without having an agenda and radiating the compassionate, ever-present love of God. She offers people the permission to be exactly as they are, without having to varnish their speech with platitudes or wear religious masks.

Insight. Because introverts tend to observe before entering into conversations and experiences, we often possess insight that others who have thrown themselves into the center of the action might not have. Our wisdom is born of observation and reflection. I've often thought that if someone were to write me into a story, I wouldn't be the protagonist or antagonist, or even a major character, I would be the narrator. Since I enjoy observing from the sidelines, I have a wide-angle view of the characters and the plot movements that the figures in the center of the story don't always have.

Some of introverts' insight originates from self-understanding, which develops as we go deeper into the workings of our internal worlds. Our time spent in solitude and reflection opens a window into our soul and we can become quite articulate about our thoughts and feelings. Those who model self-awareness can be of great benefit to others, who might not be as capable of putting their experiences and thoughts into words.

Many introverts also have intuitive powers that enable them to see below the surface and to cut through the layers that separate a person from self-understanding. Even if some introverts do not have an inborn intuition, they can develop an ability to perceive on deep levels because they have a high degree of self-perception. One introverted pastor I know has earned the nickname "The Razor" because of his ability to pierce the walls of others and help them see things about themselves they had not seen before. This gift of insight can also be valuable when we observe patterns in relationships or group dynamics. Those who are sensitive to their emotions can often gauge the underlying emotional climate of a person or group and reflect on it at appropriate times.

An extroverted missionary friend of mine was part of an organization that was led by an introverted director. My friend said, "We would spend two hours talking and going back and forth, and he wouldn't say a word. But at the end, when the rest of us were lost and exhausted, he would say three sentences that would perfectly capture the essence of what were talking about. We would then see with total clarity what had been the importance of the conversation. He would say more in ten seconds than the rest of us had said in an afternoon."

Listening and giving space. It is difficult to overestimate the power of genuine listening. Good listening can change the world. Listening is not only a means to the end of greater understanding. Listening itself communicates the value of the other person and his thoughts, so the act of listening is itself an act of love. We live in a culture where people are rarely listened to. Our families, workplaces and churches are the battlegrounds of what I call "the extroverted thrust and parry." Conversations become competitions. One person leads with a statement or a story, but another person averts the blow and immediately counters with a story of their own, which is only tangentially related to the first move. The duel is joined by others and it proceeds on, but no one ever scores any points. In this sequence, no one is actually listened to and treated as having something worthwhile to say.

Introverts are natural listeners because of their internal processing mechanism, yet listening is still something that must be cultivated. There is a vast difference between merely not speaking and genuine listening. True listening requires us to silence the constant monologue running through our heads. We must also develop the skills of asking good questions and listening not only to the words being said but to the thoughts and feelings behind them.

Related to listening is something that a mentor of mine described as "giving space" to people. Each person takes up a certain amount of "space." That space has physical, emotional and intellectual qualities, but it also has more abstract attributes related to charisma, authority and sway with a group of people. Space in a particular setting has a zero sum gain, so people regularly compete with one another for space. People who talk a lot occupy more space than people who talk less, so introverts often take up less space, which means they have space to give others. Giving space to others, whether to talk, think silently, express doubts and feelings, take action, or do nothing, gives others the rare gift of letting them be exactly as they are.

I didn't truly learn the value of listening and giving space to others until I became a chaplain. The memory of my first death visit stands out to me. I was the chaplain on call at a hospital in Orange County, California, and I received a message from the ICU nurse that an elderly woman was about to die. When I arrived, I was surprised to find ten of her family members at her bedside. It was eerily silent. We stood there together, watching this woman take her last breaths. Every so often someone would speak to me, telling me what they loved about her and how they felt about being there. Occasionally I would ask a question to help them express their feelings. We kept vigil together for an hour and a half, until her heart stopped beating. In the time I was there, I might have said fifty words. The next week, I received a thank-you note in my mailbox. It said "You will never know how much it meant to us that you were there when nana died. You are a part of our family now."

Creativity. The connection that introverts have to their inner worlds often produces a great deal of creativity and imagination. As they search for meaning, they find sparks of God's creativity within themselves. Introverted artists, musicians, songwriters or poets are often less reliant on established patterns and thus are able to create new things. It was no coincidence that, as a college pastor, when I asked our community of students to decorate the sterile environment of the auditorium we met in for worship, the two who came forward were among the most introverted students. Though strikingly quiet in group settings, they expressed themselves profoundly through art. They created paintings and designs that helped to usher the community into the worship of God.

Loyalty. Though introverts often struggle through the steps of building friendships, once they achieve familiarity and intimacy with others they are loyal friends. Introverts have high standards of friendship and do not regularly consider acquaintances or co-workers to be among their circle of friends. I have many acquaintances but I only consider five or six people to be close friends. Introverts treasure the close relationships they have stretched so much to make, and will dedicate themselves to keeping them and nurturing them.

Introverts bring the same loyalty to their communities. When I was the pastor of a Sunday-night service, tailored toward postmodern generations, the bulk of our committed members were introverts. Many of the extroverts floated in and out, depending on the other events on their social calendar, but week after week (except when they needed to spiral out) the introverts faithfully showed up, eager to worship and to reconnect with one another. We weren't very successful on the whole at outreach, but our community was intimate and spiritually rich.

Service. Another gift I noticed about the introverts in that community was how eager they were to volunteer for tasks that took place behind the scenes. When I would preach on Jesus as servant, whether in humbling himself to take human form or in donning a towel to wash the disciples' feet, there was strong resonance among the introverts in the room. Running a contemporary worship service requires all kinds of audiovisual setup, and anyone who has participated in one knows the constant frustration of finding volunteers. But for the two years I led, I don't remember a single Sunday of scrambling to find helpers. Many of the introverts enjoyed those roles, and they felt needed and valued in their contributions. I remember being startled one Sunday to learn that for months Hilary, an introvert with a quiet passion for Jesus, had been coordinating the snacks and drinks for the community time that followed the service. She had never mentioned it to me and had never complained about it.

Calming presence. All these introverted gifts emerge as we, as introverts, come to embrace our God-given identities and the necessary roles we have to play with others. I think this is particularly true with this last gift. Introverts often give off the *appearance* of calmness, while self-doubt and social anxiety rumbles around inside of us. But those introverts whose inner worlds truly match their outer appearances are among the rarest people in the world. Psychologist Marti Olsen Laney said that one of the most significant gifts introverts have to offer extroverts is that they "help them slow down."[7] Introverts move a little slower, speak a little less and rest a little more. The extroverts in our lives, those who have taken the time to understand introverts, benefit from our lifestyle by learning that they are not defined by their activities or productivity. Introverts convey restfulness and peacefulness, which creeps into the lives of others and into our communities. There is an equanimity to us that often makes us approachable and calm under pressure.

When I worked with InterVarsity Christian Fellowship, there were four or five introverts among approximately fifty staff workers in the Los Angeles area. The saving grace for me was one older, introverted staff worker named Derek who had been with the organization for a long time. Twenty years of ministry experience as a missionary, leader and pastor to other staff workers had produced wisdom, and decades of going deep in his relationship with Jesus had borne the fruit of peacefulness that overflowed to everyone he pastored. Derek talks softly, slowly and thoughtfully. He has a quietness of soul. I remember one extroverted staff worker saying, "I love being around him, because just in standing near him, I feel more at peace."

GETTING INVOLVED IN COMMUNITY

Introverts may desire to meet people and get involved in community, but we may lack the expertise and social stamina to take the extroverted path into a community. We may find ourselves floundering on the edges. When I was a college pastor, I found myself frequently giving advice to introverted college students who wished to build relationships in the community but did not know what steps to take. There is, of course, no set formula that will apply to everyone, nor any substitute for experience, but there are a few things we can do to help build relationships and increase our level of participation in the community.

Make friends in high places. Introverts are served by channeling our social energies into shrewd and purposeful actions and relationships. One strategy is to make friends in high places. Instead of wearing ourselves out meeting different strangers in the pews every week, we can search out those people who are well connected in the community. These people may be pastors, lay leaders, greeters, members of the evangelism team or socialites in the community; basically, look for someone who is approachable and eager to meet new people. When we introduce ourselves to that person, preferably in a one-on-one setting, we can express our interests and our desire to meet others, and then we can allow them to network on our behalf and introduce us to others.

After nine months as a hospice chaplain, I had solid relationships with many of my patients but still felt like an outsider in the office. I particularly wanted to develop friendships with the social workers, so I identified the one who was the heart of the group, a highly extroverted and approachable woman named Ellie. For several weeks, I made efforts to talk to Ellie when I saw her. I asked questions about her work and life, and I was genuinely interested in the answers. After a few conversations I expressed a desire to meet some of the other social workers. She then proceeded to give me inroads with others and to include me in group conversations. Within four months, I was friends with several of them, far more at ease in the office and happier at work.

Find mentors. Searching out mentors is another way introverts can develop meaningful relationships. All the introverts I know who have been truly successful in community life have mentors who have invested in them, encouraged them and challenged them. Mentoring usually does not involve the elusive "ideal" mentor who can guide you in all aspects of personal and professional life, though we might be tempted to search for this person. Mentoring entails a variety of relationships with differing degrees of intensity.[8] Over the years I have found mentors who have helped me in various fields: discipleship, friendship, prayer, pastoring, writing, academics. Mentoring is helpful for introverts because it involves a specific, purposeful and structured relationship.

Play a role. When introverts assume a role in the community, some of the obstacles toward a sense of belonging are eased. A role or position, instead of being intimidating, can be empowering for introverts seeking to meet others and grow more comfortable. A role can give us a sense of purpose and ownership in our community, as we move from onlooker to participant, and we can also give ourselves permission to be outgoing for a set period of time as we're fulfilling our role. Depending on interests and comfort level, one could join the audiovisual team, become a greeter (for socially confident introverts), join a service team, a deacons' team or another specialized ministry of the church. For me, being the pastor or recognized leader in the community has made it far easier for me to meet people. This is true because (1) I'm expected to reach out to others and this motivates me, and (2) people introduce themselves to me.

Join a group. While some introverts are attracted to smaller communities, others are drawn to the resources and anonymity of larger churches. However, the latter struggle when they want to cultivate intimate relationships in their community, because introverts develop connections through regular interaction with the same people over time. Joining a group is an effective way to find the sense of community we desire. For some, the traditional small group structure is desirable, but for others small groups centered around building relationships feel strained. Introverts may find greater satisfaction in participating in groups that have more limited parameters and a focused goal. Consider participating in a task-oriented committee, starting a writer's group or a book club, or joining with people who are reaching out to the homeless or others who are on the outside of your surrounding communities. Pay attention to what you feel called to, and find a group that fits your passions, contributions and specific skill set. Shared experiences draw people together and facilitate conversation, and organic relationships develop as you discover commonalities with others.

Socialize with a purpose. My friend Susan says that nothing is as taxing to her as small talk. She compares it to a dance, in which you step lively through the trivial topics of the day, matching the rhythms of your conversation partners with news, stories and wit. When it comes to conversational grace, many introverts have two left feet. Our need to think before we speak slows the pace of our repartee, and by the time we have a contribution to make, the conversation may have already moved on to the next topic. For some introverts, small talk is so uncomfortable that they consciously avoid social situations. I remember one man telling me that he would leave church services a few minutes before they ended in order to avoid the agony of the fellowship hour. But the reality is that small talk is essential for building relationships; in small talk, we establish initial connections with others that we may wish to pursue further.

I advise introverts to have a goal to their socializing. Instead of being bounced around the room like a social pinball, approach people with a purpose. Learn the backgrounds of a few people who will be at your social event and engage them in conversation about a shared interest. Or, more simply, just have a question to ask, a problem to solve or a favor to request. For example, find someone who can help you with your career or with your golf swing. For some who are particularly tormented by unstructured social events, having a semiprepared script helps ease the stress of small talk. Do some research on the day's news. Think of the questions you like to be asked. Rehearse open-ended conversation starters or interesting responses to inevitable questions such as "What do you do?"

Reveal your process. A common complaint I hear from friends and colleagues is that I don't let them into the inner workings of my mind and emotions. I process internally until I reach a verdict, and then I will present to them the conclusions or decisions I have arrived at. The problem is that the bonds of intimacy are built in the uncertainty, open-endedness and messiness of our process. It's in the process that we are most vulnerable, and if we allow others that we trust to see those parts of us, we find deep connection and empathy with each other. We allow others to participate in our decisions, and on the deepest levels, we begin to share our lives with each other and to have our hearts woven together.

Be available. Put yourself in situations where you are interacting with others. Angle your body toward others, look them in the eyes and greet people by name.

Ask questions. Asking questions is the surest vehicle toward building relationships. Many people enjoy talking about themselves, and asking questions will get them started. Furthermore, asking questions relieves introverts from doing most of the talking. Start with basic questions about daily life and work, then gradually move on to deeper questions about family and personal dreams as you become more comfortable with a person. I've found that I can have a conversation on almost any topic with anyone by asking good questions.

Overexpress yourself. Introverts are often misunderstood or mislabeled because their internal processing generates a stoic façade on the outside. To counter that, consciously "overexpress" yourself: smile, laugh, nod, shake your head and make encouraging listening sounds ("Hmm," "Huh," "Oh," etc.). Beware of "the introverted stare" (merely looking at the person talking with your head tilted to the side without giving any feedback).

Look for who is initiating with you. As you are attempting to develop relationships, who are those people who are making similar attempts to build relationships with you? Who is asking you questions and showing interest in your life? Often these people are worth investing in.

RELATIONAL CHALLENGES

The introverted road into community and relationships is not often smooth. Even after introverts progress into a community and establish relationships with others, there are relational pitfalls that can ensnare us.

Enmeshment. The first is what psychologists call "enmeshment." This is when our identities become intertwined with the identities of others, and our sense of self is distorted or absorbed into another person. Given the introverted tendency toward fewer, more intimate relationships, enmeshment is a clear danger. Younger introverts, with less experience in relationships, are particularly susceptible to unhealthy attachments to others. Romantic relationships are the most common arena of codependence, but enmeshment can occur in any relationship. Symptoms of enmeshment include spending excessive amounts of time with one person, isolation from others who were once important to you, and a sense of confusion about what you individually think and feel.

One-directional relationships. The second pitfall is falling into relationship patterns that are imbalanced and one-directional. Because introverts are typically good listeners and, at least, have the appearance of calmness, we are attractive to emotionally needy people. Introverts, gratified that other people are initiating with them, can easily get caught in these exhausting and unsatisfying relationships. An introverted friend of mine, at the suggestion of her therapist, drew a diagram of the things in her life that took energy and the things in her life that provided energy. She was surprised to find that the vast majority of her relationships stripped energy from her. She played the supportive role with her friends and family, who leaned on her as their "rock." She had to make choices to invest more energy in relationships with people who reciprocated with her.

Introverts in conflict. A reason introverts are wary of community is because relationships and group dynamics invariably involve conflict. The authors of *Type Talk at Work,* Otto Kroeger, Janet Thuesen and Hile Rutledge, remark that in conflict introverts are "yielding home-field advantage," because conflict involves verbal confrontation and introverts do not think as well on their feet as extroverts. The authors imagine introverts, embroiled in conflict, saying to themselves: "Go inside and work carefully on your next move. Don't expose yourself, don't make a fool of yourself, and don't say or do something you will regret. Above all, stay aloof, cool, and quiet."[9] While that statement is somewhat exaggerated, it is true that many introverts are conflict avoidant and that we will retreat into ourselves when tension arises. Although we may play out mental fantasies of triumphing over a verbal sparring partner, or we may work out solutions to the thorniest problems in our heads, we are not always prepared to resolve conflict with another person.

Introverts, however, do have great strengths to bring into conflicted situations. We are often composed and calm, which can prevent a situation from escalating. More often than not, the first thing out of a person's mouth in conflict is venom, but introverts' internal processing helps prevent us from saying things we will regret. Frankly, something as potentially incendiary as conflict and something as significant as relationships require delicacy and discretion. Extroverts who are reactionary could do well to learn from the example of introverts who approach conflict with more thought and diplomacy. I am convinced that James had situations of conflict in mind when he said "be quick to listen, slow to speak, slow to anger" (Jas 1:19).

When introverts are in conflict with each other, though, it may require a map in order to follow all the silences, nonverbal cues and passive-aggressive behaviors! Most of the time, introverts will do well to bypass the guesswork and give voice to their inner rumblings, even if they are incomplete and might come out inarticulately. Holding in our grievances only builds pressure and can lead to angry explosions if we do not release them. If direct conversation is inappropriate or untimely, we need to find pressure valves, such as prayer or talking things through with a close friend.

For me, conflict has been much more common in my relationships with extroverts. Extroverts are more draining for me than introverts, as they may have a more energetic presence and require more attention. Therefore, extroverts are more likely to see me struggling with irritability and shortness of speech, which can produce conflict situations. An additional trigger point for extroverts with me can be my silences or seeming inexpressiveness. Into those vacuums, they are liable to insert all kinds of assumptions and interpretations. Their frustrations are sometimes on target, however, and I find myself rightly challenged to speak my minds around them.

Yet, while extroverts may find me inscrutable, I struggle to understand the extroverted propensity to blurt things out and then act surprised when I want to hold them to what they've said. Sometimes I am shocked at what comes out of the unfiltered processing of the extroverted mind, things that would be unfathomable for me to utter because I so carefully measure my words in conflict. I have to remind myself that extroverts are prone to say things that they have not considered carefully and I need to give them the room, and the forgiveness, to take back those things.

This ability requires a healthy sense of self and a humble assertiveness. Archibald Hart, in his classic work on clergy depression, astutely observes that too many pastors (and I would apply this to all introverts), "erroneously call their inability to stand up for themselves 'Christian humility.' " Hart clarifies that "healthy assertiveness means, very simply that people can stand up for themselves without feeling guilty, refuse to let others manipulate them or impose their wills on them, express their feelings in a non-hostile manner, refuse to be intimidated, and confront conflict courageously."[10]

To "confront conflict courageously" does not mean that we strike when we see other people's vulnerability. Rather, confronting conflict courageously likely involves two steps. First, we genuinely *listen* to people. It takes tremendous courage and a healthy sense of self to give people the space to voice their complaints about us, so our ability to listen is the most important skill for neutralizing a hostile crowd. The sort of listening I refer to is not just allowing people to vent but also listening for new insight about the situation, the other people and yourself.[11] When you listen, you might gain a new perspective, and by virtue of your listening, the other people's feelings may change about the situation—even if the circumstances remain the same—because they will sense that their opinion has been honestly heard. Listening first often enables the other people to listen to us when it is our turn. I continue to be amazed at how disarming it can be if we genuinely listen to other people, especially since this is often the unexpected response.

The second part of confronting conflict courageously is *asserting ourselves*. This means that we will express ourselves in clear yet tactful ways, focusing on our own experiences, thoughts and feelings—rather than on the actions and words of the other person. Preparation will help introverts for these sorts of conversations. Writing down our thoughts or discussing them with another person prior to the interaction will bring clarity and reduce anxiety.

Technology and relationships. It may be that introverts are recipients both of the greatest benefits and the greatest liabilities of modern technology. From a positive end, the Internet offers us opportunities for relationships that do not require as much of us as in-person contact does. It offers us the frequency and level of interaction that many of us do not have the energy to pursue regularly in other venues. E-mail, in particular, allows us to think before we communicate, to correspond at our own pace and to change what we say before we send it. E-mail doesn't make the immediate social demands that cell phones do, and it enables us to communicate without interruption. In addition, there is a degree of distance in communication via e-mail, and this distance frees us to be more vulnerable than we might normally be. In a similar way, there is an anonymity to online relationships; for example, blogs and networking websites enable us to express our inner thoughts to others from the privacy of our own homes, again using the written word, which is usually our the preferred method of communication. Finally, in other benefits, technology enables some of us to employ our creativity and imagination in graphic and visual displays. Other times our handheld technology can help us carve out niches of solitude. My friend Jessica says she finds social respite in her "iPod-created bubble."

But the effects of technology are not all favorable for introverts. The ubiquity of personal technology gives others the expectation that we are always available. Cell phones, text messages and e-mails can demand our immediate attention and distract us from the necessary and important work of internal reflection, which grounds us and gives us strength. A more subtle danger is that our technology allures us with the *illusion* of intimacy but not the reality of it. We may be regularly communicating with others and yet painfully alone. Shane Hipps, author of *The Hidden Power of Electronic Culture* and *Flickering Pixels,* says that "if your relationships are comprised of a disproportionate amount of mediated communication you will be relationally, spiritually and emotional malnourished."[12] Technology can become for us a hiding place, a drug we take to escape from our negative emotions and experiences. It can expose the shadow side of our imaginations, taking us into a nameless fantasy world where we can feed our addictions, all the while aggravating our sense of isolation from others, God and, even, ourselves. We must become aware of these traps of modern technology and use its immense benefits without letting it overpower us.

AN INTROVERT SUCCEEDING IN COMMUNITY

Roy is a thirty-six-year-old introvert who lives in Orange County, California. Contemplative and thoughtful, he feels less connected to God when he doesn't have time to think. He enjoys being around others, especially when he does not feel pressured to talk. Roy's closest friendships originated in high school and college, and when he meets with groups of friends, he will interject a few comments into the conversations but mostly prefers to listen. He describes his friendships as "deep but fairly controlled." He lives in the same house as a married couple, and though he likes living with his friends, he finds the social interaction to be wearying and, at times, invasive.

He is an assistant professor of mathematics at a local college, and he prefers to spend his lunch hours perched on the quad, surrounded by students but not talking to them, rather than in the privacy of his office. He prepares extensively before each class but does not always feel the need to write his thoughts down. Roy relishes opportunities to teach in the classroom setting but also enjoys tutoring students in one-on-one contexts. As an active participant in local government and in a tutoring program in a nearby, lower class community, he finds networking among diverse groups to be very comfortable, calling it "goal-oriented socializing."

As an Armenian, he is one of the few minorities who attend a large, evangelical Presbyterian church in the area. He began attending this church as a high school junior, when he became a regular in the back pews of weekly worship services. In the next few years, he joined a wind ensemble in the church and also began to participate in the college fellowship, but he reported that he "wasn't going for the friendships but because it was the right thing to do." While the other college students would play basketball outside after their meetings, Roy would stay in the room, playing the piano and singing hymns. His college pastor noticed him and challenged him to be less isolated from others, which led Roy to attend more social events even though he never felt close to the other students.

Overall, Roy prefers relationships that are task oriented, rather than conversation based, so as he continued attending the church, he joined several committees and was also part of a planning team that started a new worship service oriented toward younger generations. He mostly enjoys working behind the scenes, setting up chairs and audio equipment for worship services. He discovered that he likes the structured format of committee meetings, which are driven by tight agendas. He eventually became interested in the decision-making process at the church, so he participated in a class for those interested in church leadership. Through the relationships he established in the committees and the other activities he is a part of, Roy was elected as an elder in the church when he was thirty-one. People recognized his deep faith, his thoughtfulness, his commitment to the community and the different perspectives he brought. Ever the introvert, though, after evening meetings he will often stay up late processing what they have discussed, replaying the topics and interactions in his head. After he stepped into church leadership, he accepted the role of weekly emcee at the new worship service and has quickly became a highly recognized and beloved member of that community.

6

The Ability to Lead

" 'Leadership personality,' 'leadership style' and 'leadership traits' do not exist. Among the most effective leaders I have encountered and worked with in a half century, some locked themselves into their office and others were ultragregarious. . . . Some were quick and impulsive; others studied and studied again and took forever to come to a decision. Some were warm and instantly 'simpatico'; others remained aloof even after years of working closely with others, not only with outsiders like me but with the people with their own organization. . . . The one and only personality trait the effective ones I have encountered have in common was something they did not have: they had little or no 'charisma' and little use either for the term or what it signifies."

PETER DRUCKER, IN THE FOREWORD TO *THE LEADER OF THE FUTURE: NEW VISIONS, STRATEGIES AND PRACTICES FOR THE NEXT ERA*

The senior pastor and I walked into the church office at the same time that Tuesday morning. He had been in ministry at the large Presbyterian church for five years, whereas I had been a minister to collegians and young adults for nine months. As we opened the sparkling glass door to a new week, we were greeted in the lobby by two-silver haired women who were there to fold bulletins for the upcoming Sunday. At the sight of the senior pastor, their faces lit up and they quickly interposed themselves between him and the door to the pastors' offices. For fifteen minutes they exchanged pleasantries, the women lavishing praise on him for the previous Sunday's sermon and spinning their well-rehearsed tales of hip replacements and winter arthritis. Reluctantly, the women returned to their bulletin-origami duties, and the senior pastor paraded through the office hallway, sharing extended greetings and weekend reflections with each member of the administrative staff.

Meanwhile, I had ducked the women and made it through the door unnoticed. I gave a running hello to the receptionist and took shelter in the haven of my office, where I was eager to delve into John Calvin's *Institutes of the Christian Religion* during the half hour before our staff meeting. Through my closed, frustratingly hollow door, I could hear each conversation about vacation cabins, new outfits, the abnormally cold weather for southern California and the new brand of church coffee (which was still terrible). As I tried to concentrate on Calvin's doctrine of the Holy Spirit and how I might use it in my Sunday evening sermon, a different indwelling voice began to pepper me with familiar questions: *Is* that *what a pastor is supposed to be like? Does the staff think I am withdrawn or antisocial? Am I in the right business? Why is it that churches spend millions of dollars on new buildings but can't buy decent coffee?* (The last question may not be particular to introverts.)

There may be no other feature of American life that contains as much bias toward extroversion as leadership. Since our leaders epitomize our cultural values, it is no surprise that Americans want their leaders to be extroverts. Psychologist and author Marti Olsen Laney cites a study that was repeated three times with the same findings: "[Both introverts and extroverts] were asked if they would prefer their ideal leaders to be introverted or extroverted.

Reflecting the prejudices in our culture, both introverts and extroverts choose extroverts as their ideal self and ideal leader."[1] Clinical psychologist Leonard Holmes, in analyzing American presidents from the last two centuries, found that "Great presidents were not only stubborn and disagreeable, but were also more extroverted, open to experience, assertive, achievement striving, excitement seeking, and more open to fantasy."[2] The tendency toward extroverted presidents has increased in recent decades, as the role of media and the importance of knowing how to utilize the media have become central to winning elections.

"IDEAL" LEADERSHIP TRAITS

Richard Daft, author of the business textbook *The Leadership Experience,* cites numerous studies that have sifted out five attributes of successful leaders, called the "Big Five personality dimensions": openness to experience, emotional stability, conscientiousness, agreeableness and extroversion. Although Daft insists there is no one leadership model and that people of all personality types can lead effectively, he cites the findings of one leadership study: "One recent summary of more than seventy years of personality and leadership research did find evidence that four of the five dimensions were consistently related to successful leadership. The researchers found considerable evidence that people who score high on the dimensions of extroversion, agreeableness, conscientiousness, and emotional stability are more successful leaders."[3]

Though leadership paradigms practiced both in the corporate world and in the church have shifted in the last twenty years, leadership stereotypes endure. Our collective cultural subconscious holds to a particular mold of leadership, so many of us either disqualify ourselves or others based on the following four criteria.

Charisma. For many people charisma is the preeminent trait that distinguishes a great leader from ordinary people. It is an intangible quality—perhaps better described than defined—that attracts others to a leader like a magnet. Charismatic leaders have a theatrical quality to them, and they relish playing the lead role amidst other actors on the stage. Public attention is an intoxicating force that brings out their best qualities. They are able to inspire and captivate others with their passion and presence.

President John F. Kennedy was laced with charisma. An article written a few years ago recalled Kennedy's visit and speech to the people of Tampa Bay in 1963: "Though he spoke on the economic conditions of the country for 20 minutes instead of the scheduled five, no one really heard what he said—only how he said it. The audience was mesmerized." A motorcycle officer who escorted the presidential motorcade gushed: "I remember as he shook our hands he looked us in the eye and said each of our names. It was thrilling. I didn't wash my hand for a week."[4] People with charisma have the uncanny ability, as my friend describes them, "to speak to millions but make you feel like they're speaking just to you. You don't know them, and you'll never meet them, but they feel like your friends." A truly charismatic leader has a mystical ability to mix the appearance of an untouchable, larger-than-life persona and an accessible, sympathetic friend.

Dominance. People who are dominant are hard-charging, persuasive and directive. They can motivate people and accomplish their goals by the sheer force of their will. This trait is primarily *positional,* meaning that dominant leaders rely on the authority of rank or title to compel others.[5] Their understanding of leadership "assumes that humans are naturally still, at rest, and that they need some motivating force to get them going."[6]

When I think of a dominant leader I think of an extroverted pastor I once met who has built a large and successful youth ministry. He has positioned himself at the heart of the program, to the point that people cannot conceive of the ministry without him. He is constantly pushing things forward, starting new programs and rallying people around his ideas. He will not take no for an answer, and will debate and persuade until the other person relents or ends the conversation.

Gregariousness. Gregarious leaders relate comfortably with people of different personalities and backgrounds. They are able to initiate and prolong conversations and are at home among strangers. They have the capacity to disarm people and assuage conflict with their warmth and charm. Gregarious leaders in the Christian community are the face of a welcoming, friendly, inviting church. They set the tone for hospitality and openness among the congregation. They are skilled in the ministry of chat, filling awkward silences with engaging conversation, and people feel quickly at ease around them.

In a highly verbal culture, words carry power. The person who wields words with the greatest fluency, or even just uses the most words, is invested with authority. In group contexts people often give leadership to those who are most willing to present their opinions, even though their solutions may not be the right or best ones. Speaking is construed as confidence whereas reserving one's opinion, or only speaking up on topics one has previously considered, is interpreted as timidity or deference to others.

J. Oswald Sanders, in his popular book *Spiritual Leadership,* describes the apostle Paul in a strikingly extroverted way: "You can measure leaders by the number and the quality of their friends. Judged by that measuring rod, Paul had a genius for friendship. He was essentially a gregarious man."[7] Sanders goes on to ask potential leaders if they "are at ease among strangers" as a gauge for determining whether a person has a leadership gift. Rick Warren says that preaching effectively is directly related to the accessibility of a pastor outside of the pulpit: "Be approachable. Don't hide out in your study. . . . One of the best ways to warm up a crowd is to meet as many people as you can before you speak to them. Get out among the crowd and talk to people. It shows you are interested in them personally. Many pastors like to gather their staff or

key leaders in a private room before the service and pray while the
people are coming in. I believe you ought to pray for your service
at some other time. Don't miss an opportunity to be with people
when you have the chance."[8]

Superstardom. The superstar leader is one who excels at everything. Anyone with church leadership experience knows that the
tasks of leading are manifold, even to the point of contradiction.
Those in charge are called on to provide visionary, intellectual,
administrative, financial, social, spiritual and emotional leadership. Superstar leaders are able to successfully address both the
large needs of the organization and the particular, more delicate
needs of the individuals who comprise the organization. They
have a rare combination of skills, which are often bolstered by
intangibles like charisma and high energy, and are able to assert
those qualities in a variety of settings.

Roy Oswald and Otto Kroeger, authors of *Personality Type and
Religious Leadership,* provide a dizzying list of the tasks congregations expect clergy to be proficient in

- leading in worship

- preparing and delivering sermons

- teaching both adults and children

- visiting the sick, bereaved and dying

- accepting outside speaking engagements

- administering the church office

- conflict resolution/building harmony with the parish

- visiting and recruiting new members

- counseling persons with personal difficulties

- representing the parish in ecumenical affairs

- engaging in continuing professional and spiritual development

- assisting victims of social neglect, injustice and prejudice
- youth ministry
- baptizing, marrying and conducting funerals
- leading fundraising drives
- participating in denominational activities
- fostering fellowship within the parish
- leading in parish goal setting and helping in its implementation
- recruiting and training parish leaders
- visiting people in their homes
- promoting enthusiasm for parish activities[9]

One pastor I interviewed said that her congregation expects her to be good at all things, to lead in every situation, no matter what the circumstances, and to always be available. Another friend, who is a solo pastor in the northeast, agreed: "Most church cultures have expectations for pastors that no single person could ever fulfill. They want sermons that are biblical, deep, thoughtful and well prepared, but they also want the outgoing, extroverted, people-person, as well as the CEO mover and shaker. These seldom come in one person. This may be one reason why so many drop out of pastoral ministry in five or ten years."

In reviewing the qualifications we look for in leaders, I'm left to echo George Barna's question, "Who could possibly meet such a wide range of disparate expectations?"[10] We set our leaders up for inevitable failure when we measure them by unreachable standards.[11] So this is not simply a matter of whether extroverts or introverts make better leaders, this is a question about the general soundness of our leadership models. When we explicitly or implicitly communicate that only a few people, for whom the stars miraculously align, can lead with power and effectiveness, we discourage those who do not fit our cultural ideals but have great potential to lead, thus doing harm to the body of Christ. Further, this model of leadership only validates the common, unbiblical expectation that pastors play the role of benefactor while everyone else in the congregation is a beneficiary.

THE GOOD NEWS

While these characteristics of the "ideal" Western leader pivot around the personality of a leader and while it is glaringly clear that they favor extroversion over introversion, there is good news: the stereotypical leadership mold is breaking. Our old models are fading into obsolescence. The long-term sustainability of an organization or a church cannot depend on the personality features of the central leader, no matter how captivating or compelling that person is. In discussions in the corporate world, in classrooms and in the church, we are reconsidering the qualities that makeup a successful leader.

Level 5 leadership. Jim Collins's book *Good to Great* is a landmark study that has shattered preexisting paradigms of executive leadership. Collins discovered that glitzy, dynamic, high-profile CEOs are actually a *hindrance* to the long-term success of their corporations. Charismatic leaders naturally attract people, but these leaders may be less effective at drawing people to the mission and values of the organization itself.[12] No one embodied the larger-than-life executive more than Lee Iacocca, Chrysler's icon in the 1980s. He almost single-handedly steered his car company away from disaster and put it on the road to prosperity. He reveled in the spotlight, and his celebrity status rose at times to the level of a rock star—to the point where he considered pursuing a presidential nomination. Yet after Iacocca's retirement, Chrysler's profits faltered and it was sold to a German rival carmaker just five years later. Iacocca, more concerned with personal reputation than company sustainability, had done little to invest in his successors or to ensure the longevity of Chrysler.

In sharp contrast, Collins presents the story of Colman Mockler, the CEO of Gillette from 1975 to 1991. Mockler made personal sacrifices and took substantial risks for the long-term success of the company and the profits of the shareholders, and he was so effective that $1 invested in Gillette in December 1976 was worth $95.68 in December 1996. Laconic and reserved, Mockler labored in relative anonymity for a big-time executive; he was a man who prioritized the success of his company over ego gratification.

Mockler and executives like him are examples of what Collins calls "Level 5 Leaders."[13] In his key points, he summarizes the characteristics of this type of leader:

- Level 5 leaders display compelling modesty, are self-effacing and understated. In contrast, two-thirds of the comparison companies had leaders with gargantuan personal egos, which contributed to the demise or continued mediocrity of the companies.

- Level 5 leaders display a workmanlike diligence—more plow horse than show horse.

- Level 5 leaders set up their successors for even greater success in the next generation, whereas egocentric level 4 leaders often set up their successors for failure.[14]

Collins also asserts that "one of the most damaging trends in recent history is the tendency to select dazzling, celebrity leaders and to de-select potential Level 5 leaders."[15]

In commending humility, self-sacrifice and a commitment to the organization over personal glory, Collins finds himself in the heart of an ancient tradition of leadership: the biblical picture of the servant leader. The authors of the New Testament caution us against those leaders who are heavy on allure and light on humility. Scripture subverts our cultural tendency to identify leaders by glamorous personality features and instead points us toward people who are faithful servants of God and others. These people are willing to become the least so that others will know the self-sacrificing love of God. Servant leaders return again and again to the model of Jesus, who on his last night, took a towel and scraped the dirt off the scaly feet of his nomadic followers. The route to his coronation as King of kings went outside the walls of the holy city to a jagged Roman cross. Jesus used his immeasurable power and knowledge of God, not for his own aggrandizement but so that others might see the glory and salvation of God.

Character over charisma. While charisma has a magnetic force to it, its power can be fleeting. Unless it is buttressed by substance and consistency, its pull fades quickly. Leadership guru Peter Drucker said "Indeed, charisma becomes the undoing of leaders. It makes them inflexible, convinced of their own infallibility, unable to change."[16] For that reason contemporary leadership discussions are elevating *character* over charisma.

Character in a leader is the quality that has the ability not only to draw others but also to maintain their loyalty. *Character* is more than personal integrity and ethical decision-making, though it certainly includes those elements. The central component of character is authenticity. Someone with character acts in unison with his or her God-given nature. Characterless leaders are tossed between the waves of personal success and popularity with others, and they often lose their true selves in the process. Leaders with character find their identity from within and in harmony with whom God has uniquely created them to be.

It cannot be overemphasized that the biblical descriptions of leadership do not include references to personality type. Instead, they consistently describe leaders as people of admirable and consistent character:

> I left you behind in Crete for this reason, so that you should put in order what remained to be done, and should appoint

elders in every town, as I directed you: someone who is blameless, married only once, whose children are believers, not accused of debauchery and not rebellious. For a bishop, as God's steward, must be blameless; he must not be arrogant or quick-tempered or addicted to wine or violent or greedy for gain; but he must be hospitable, a lover of goodness, prudent, upright, devout, and self-controlled. (Tit 1:5-8)

Now a bishop must be above reproach, married only once, temperate, sensible, respectable, hospitable, an apt teacher, not a drunkard, not violent but gentle, not quarrelsome, and not a lover of money. He must manage his own household well, keeping his children submissive and respectful in every way—for if someone does not know how to manage his own household, how can he take care of God's church? He must not be a recent convert, or he may be puffed up with conceit and fall into the condemnation of the devil. Moreover, he must be well thought of by outsiders, so that he may not fall into disgrace and the snare of the devil. (1 Tim 3:2-7)

Now as an elder myself and a witness of the sufferings of Christ, as well as one who shares in the glory to be revealed, I exhort the elders among you to tend the flock of God that is in your charge, exercising the oversight, not under compulsion but willingly, as God would have you do it—not for sordid gain but eagerly. Do not lord it over those in your charge, but be examples to the flock. (1 Pet 5:1-3)

True leadership is not cultivated in the limelight; it's won in the trenches. Character is something that is built. Thus, the mark of godly leadership is not a magnetic personality; it is discipline, because discipline develops character.

We gain character by opening ourselves up to God's transforming power through prayer, through solidifying our most important relationships and by practicing the good habits that enable us to become the kind of people we want to be. True leaders don't lead out of who others want them to be; therefore, introverts with character will lead as introverts. We do not try to be extroverts or contort ourselves in ways our personalities are not able to go. While we seek to grow as leaders and as people, we are committed to remaining true, because one of the greatest gifts we can offer others is leading as ourselves. People desperately want to know that it's possible to live, act and work as they are, and introverted leaders who model authenticity will give others freedom to be themselves.

The learning organization. Another movement that is changing the face of contemporary leadership is the "learning organization." Peter Senge, author of *The Fifth Discipline,* contends that in a rapid-fire, information-driven, technology-powered world, success is contingent on our individual and corporate abilities to adjust, adapt and learn.[17] The learning organization, therefore, must incorporate processes of reflection and evaluation into their organizational systems. Leaders must commit to their own learning and to fostering an environment of learning in their organizations. Thus people who think before they act and listen before they talk can be very effective leaders. The reflective, thoughtful person may be able to learn, and encourage learning, in ways that people who can't stop talking are not able to.

Even more encouraging for introverted leaders is what Chris Argyris, emeritus professor at the Harvard Business School, calls "double loop learning." He explains that the learning trajectory must move in two directions:

> Most people define learning too narrowly as mere "problem solving," so they focus on identifying and correcting errors in the external environment. Solving problems is important.

But if learning is to persist, managers and employees must also look inward. They need to reflect critically on their own behavior, identifying the ways they often inadvertently contribute to the organization's problems, and then change how they act. In particular, they must learn how the very way they go about defining and solving problems can be a source of problems in its own right.[18]

In the learning organization, successful leadership is wedded to introspection. The source of dysfunction and inefficiency in an organization may go beyond misdirected actions and strained relationships to internal motivations, tendencies and assumptions. Leaders must learn to scrutinize every aspect of their leadership and personality. People who are naturally self-reflective have a clear advantage, in this regard, as leaders of learning organizations.

Sensemaking. Another category for understanding the nature of leadership that cuts against the grain of traditional definitions is "sensemaking." Wilfred Drath and Charles Palus, at the Center for Creative Leadership, explain that "most existing theories, models, and definitions of leadership proceed from the assumption that somehow leadership is about getting people to do something."[19] Instead, Drath and Palus reimagine leadership as "the process for making sense of what people are doing together so that people will understand and be committed."[20] Leadership, in this view, is a matter of interpretation. Leaders give people a lens and a language for understanding their work and experiences in light of larger purposes. They help shape the mental frameworks of others so that those people see themselves as making contributions to the mission and direction of their organization, working in community for a common purpose.

Scott Cormode, professor of leadership development at Fuller Seminary, applies sensemaking to leadership in the church. He explains that "pastors lead by providing God's people with the theological categories to make spiritual meaning."[21] Christian leaders give people the biblical and theological tools to see their ordinary lives in the broad horizons of the kingdom of God. Sensemaking enables people to weave the disparate threads of their existence into a cohesive life of worship and discipleship. As they discover and make meaning in their individual situations, they find the freedom to think and act differently, being "transformed by the renewing of [their] minds" (Rom 12:2).

I had a difficult time understanding this idea of sensemaking until I realized that I regularly practice it with introverts who are wrestling with questions about leadership. Whether in contexts of spiritual direction, leadership training, pastoral interactions or preaching, I have worked with fellow introverts in finding a new intellectual grid for understanding leadership. We have battled against common leadership myths and told a different story about the attributes and disciplines that help a leader to thrive—and then I've helped others see their capacities to lead and insert themselves into that story.

MAKING BIBLICAL SENSE OF INTROVERTED LEADERSHIP

Leadership is not a status or a position to be attained, but it is a gift of God. The word *charisma* (broader cultural definition notwithstanding) means "gift," a tangible expression of God's grace, charged with the power of the Giver. All that we have, including the ability to lead others, is from God. Paul described his entire ministry as grace: "Of this gospel I have become a servant according to the gift of God's grace that was given me by the working of his power. Although I am the very least of all the saints, this grace was given to me to bring to the Gentiles the news of the boundless riches of Christ" (Eph 3:7-8). God's gifts are not conditional on our worthiness for receiving them or our fitness for using them, and they are certainly not conditional on personality type. God does not make sure someone is an extrovert before he bestows a gift of leadership, nor does he give gifts by mistake. And he sees his gifts, and their recipients, through to the end—granting the ability to embrace the gift and to use it for the blessing of his church.

In fact, God may even have a vested interest in giving gifts to people who seem ill-suited to possess them. God delights in reversing expectations, in choosing the most unexpected people to lead, prophesy and proclaim. He reversed the law of primogeniture by choosing the younger Jacob, over the elder Esau, to be the father of the nation of Israel. God passed over Jesse's more physically impressive sons to anoint David, the shepherd boy with delicate features, as king over Israel. The line of the Messiah came not through a pure bloodline of queens but through Rahab, a prostitute, and through Ruth, a foreigner. Jesus chose uneducated fishermen and traitorous tax collectors to be his emissaries to the ends of the earth. He himself did not ride into Jerusalem atop a white steed with a waving flag of victory, but he sauntered in on a beast of burden. God appeared to Paul, seething persecutor of Christians, and reversed the direction of his life to make him apostle to the loathsome Gentiles.

God has always been about the business of shattering expectations, and in our culture, the standards of leadership are extroverted. It perfectly follows the biblical trend that God would choose the unexpected and the culturally "unfit"—like introverts —to lead his church for the sake of his greater glory. The apostle Paul marveled at this paradox: " 'My grace is sufficient for you, for power is made perfect in weakness.' So, I will boast all the more gladly of my weaknesses, so that the power of Christ may dwell in me" (2 Cor 12:9).

INTRODUCTED LEADERS
All these contemporary leadership discussions I have reviewed above point to people who are thoughtful, reflective and eager to

learn. These people are skilled in observation and in listening, and they are able to detect patterns and nuances in themselves and others. They see the big picture and are able to hold together in their minds great amounts of information. In short, the door of the leadership world has been opened wide to introverts and the strengths they have to offer.

Though extroverts may continue to be seen as "ideal" leaders and introverts may have feelings of displacement in leadership positions, the fact is there are introverts leading in the corporate world, in nonprofit organizations and in the church. And while Richard Daft sounds surprised when he recounts that "although extroversion is often considered an important trait for a leader, leaders in the real world are about equally divided between extroverts and introverts,"[22] Elaine Aron is not surprised when she reports that introverts are often a part of the "advisor class"—those who counsel and instruct others—as compared to the "warrior class," the doers of the world who receive guidance from the advisors.[23] In fact, a recent *USA Today* article reports that four in ten top executives are introverts,[24] and in a 2006 Barna study, 24 percent of Protestant senior pastors self-identified as introverts. [25]

There are a variety of popular contemporary leaders who identify themselves as introverts and are honest about the struggles they encounter. Pastor and scholar Eugene Peterson confesses that it was difficult for him in his pastoral ministry to visit families in their homes because he is "introverted and shy."[26] Episcopal priest and celebrated preacher Barbara Brown Taylor concedes that "it can be difficult to be an introvert in the church, especially if you happen to be the pastor."[27] Postmodern pastor and entrepreneur Erwin McManus says, as an introvert, he prefers to interact with a few people *on the sides* of social gatherings.[28] Emerging church leader Brian McLaren has learned to say "no" to some requests and to take a regular sabbath in order to recharge his introverted batteries.[29] Writer and campus ministry leader Donald Miller admits that as an "extreme introvert," he finds community life challenging.[30] But all of these introverts have used their gifts to lead and edify the body of Christ. We can also look back a little further to find other introverted heroes of faith. Mother Teresa, Martin Luther King Jr. and Jonathan Edwards are people who have led in the church and in the world . . . as introverts.

Mother Teresa: Compassion as the beating heart of mission. In March 1947, Teresa pleaded with her archbishop for his permission to go to the streets of Calcutta: "Let me go, and give myself for them, let me offer myself and those who will join me for those unwanted poor, the little street children, the sick, the dying, the beggars, let me go into their very holes and bring in their broken homes the joy and peace of Christ."[31] For the next fifty years, Mother Teresa and the Missionaries of Charity sought to minister to Jesus in his "distressing disguise" of poverty and desolation. As an introvert,[32] she gave tender, personal attention to each suffering person, seeing the dignity and humanity in them where others only saw shame and death. She was convinced that if her order "brought joy to one unhappy home—made one innocent child from the street keep pure for Jesus—one dying person die in peace with God . . . it would be worth offering everything—because that one would bring great joy to the Heart of Jesus."[33]

Like many introverts, Mother Teresa led by example. Her extravagant acts of service and humility overshadowed the power of her quiet words. There was a recklessness to her courage, an audacity to her love that would not let any obstacles keep her from the people of Calcutta. She was a cheerful and enthusiastic giver, with relentless energy for caring for the sick and the poor. As she offered herself to them, she presented herself to Jesus, whom she longed to know in the most intimate ways. In the time of preparation for her ministry, she experienced mystical visions of Jesus beckoning her to be his light in the darkness. Others who saw her tender affection for him teased her as "Jesus' spoiled bride."[34]

However, it has been only recently that the world has learned of the great contradictions that existed in her soul. The woman who taught us to look for the presence of Jesus in everyone and everything spent most of her life feeling his absence. In her anguish, she wrote "The more I want Him, the less I am wanted. I want to love Him as He has not been loved, and yet there is that separation, that terrible emptiness, that feeling of absence of God."[35] The saint who went into the dark holes of the poor had caverns in her own soul, and she suffered in lonely silence, not allowing those around her into her pain.

At the same time, it was within her own spiritual darkness that she found wells of compassion for the crumpled, beautiful masses of humanity that she encountered every day. She ministered out of a broken heart. She understood firsthand that, as excruciating as physical poverty could be, it could not compare to the poverty of feeling rejected and unloved. As she agonized in a tsunami of internal turmoil, she identified with lepers, orphans and outcasts, and found a love for them that rippled around the world.

Martin Luther King Jr.: Commitment to ideals as the source of true charisma. Many may be shocked to learn that Martin Luther King Jr. was an introvert. The man who dripped with charisma and rhetorical genius, his sonorous voice sounding against the walls of racial injustice, was considered "quiet" and "reserved" in his younger days. One of his college professors reported that he was "quiet, introspective and very much introverted," and biographer David Garrow says that "most found King to be a quiet and reserved young man, 'just a regular student,' who always sat in the back of classrooms."[36] Others said that he was very studious, devoting "time to his books night and day."[37] He described himself as an "ambivert"—half introvert and half extrovert, able to "withdraw within himself for long, single minded concentration on his people's problems, and then exert the force of personality and conviction that makes him a public leader."[38]

Martin Luther King Jr. was first an intellectual and a scholar, only drawn into the spotlight by a sense of divine calling to advocate for racial justice and equality. Even though he grew up as a minister's son, King had been wary of religion, uncertain if he could square his intellectual bent with what he called the "emotionalism" of black churches. It was a personal crisis that led to his conversion. A midnight caller threatened that if King did not leave Montgomery, Alabama, they would blow up his house and his family. As he sat at his kitchen table, he prayed and "it seemed at that moment that I could hear an inner voice saying to me, 'Martin Luther, stand up for righteousness. Stand up for justice. Stand up for truth. And lo I will be with you, even until the end of the world.' . . . I heard the voice of Jesus saying still to fight on. He promised never to leave me, never to leave me alone. No never alone." He exulted that "Almost at once my fears began to go. My uncertainty disappeared."[39]

Martin Luther King Jr.'s ideals, and his unwavering commitment to them even in the face of death, were the source of his charisma—a gift from God that compelled him into his perilous mission and enabled him to articulate the hopes and dreams of his people, and all people. His passionate and poetic rhetoric gained an audience, but his ideals were what catalyzed the black movement. The method of his protest was nonviolent resistance, which he learned from Jesus and from his fellow introvert, Mahatma Gandhi. This type of civil disobedience was the fruit of the creativity, thoughtfulness and unflinching determination often found in introverts.

Jonathan Edwards: Leading with light and heat. Jonathan Edwards's notoriety issues mostly from the terrifying image of a spider suspended over a flame, an image from his infamous sermon "Sinners in the Hands of an Angry God." What few know is that that sermon, as grisly as some of its details were, was a centerpiece in the first Great Awakening, a religious revival that swept through the American colonies in the 1730s and 1740s. While some decried the religious excesses of the revival, which was marked by great emotional and physical displays of mourning sin and glorifying God's holiness, Edwards was its most articulate and thoughtful defender.

Though Edwards lived 200 years before the genesis of Jung's collective unconscious theory, I have no doubt he was an introvert. Historian John Gillies said that he, in contrast to the rhetorical fire of revivalist preacher George Whitefield, was "a preacher of low and moderate voice, a natural way of delivery, and without any agitation of body, or anything else in the manner to excite attention, except his habitual and great solemnity, looking and speaking as in the presence of God."[40] His discipline in solitude, study and writing could rival the regimen of the most trained professional soldier. During his twenty-year tenure as the pastor of the large Congregational Church of Northampton, Massachusetts, he spent thirteen hours a day in his study! An early biographer marveled that "these hours were passed, not in perusing or treasuring up the thoughts of others, but in employments far more exhausting—in the investigation of difficult subjects, in the origination and arrangement of thoughts, in the invention of arguments, and in the discovery of truths and principles."[41]

Edwards's intellectual abilities were massive. The theological treatises he penned—such as *Religious Affections, The Freedom of the Will* and *The End for Which God Created the World,* as well as his popular biography of missionary David Brainerd—have shaped the minds of countless scholars, pastors and missionaries. His model of pastor-scholar is one that many introverted leaders will naturally assume. Though his mind, which bordered on genius, is in itself remarkable, even more incredible to me is the passion that he had for knowing Jesus Christ in a personal, experiential way. For him the "light" of the mind was incomplete without the "heat" of the emotions. He explained the reason for his diligence in studying Scripture, "the more you have of a rational knowledge of divine things, the more opportunity will there be, when the Spirit shall be breathed into your heart, to see the excellency of these things, and to taste the sweetness of them."[42] Edwards spoke of a "sense" that was a way of knowing that transcended the intellect, that seemed to sweep him up in almost mystical experiences of God. In a personal narrative, he recorded this experience:

> Once, as I rode out into the woods for my health, in 1737, having alighted from my horse in a retired place, as my manner commonly has been, to walk for divine contemplation and prayer, I had a view that for me was extraordinary, of the glory of the Son of God, as Mediator between God and man, and his wonderful, great, full, pure and sweet grace and love, and meek and gentle condescension. This grace that appeared so calm and sweet, appeared also great above the heavens. The person of Christ appeared ineffably excellent with an excellency great enough to swallow up all thought and conception . . . which continued as near as I can judge, about an hour; which kept me the greater part of the time in a flood of tears, and weeping aloud. I felt an ardency of soul to be, what I know not otherwise how to express, emptied and annihilated; to lie in the dust, and to be full of Christ alone; to love him with a holy and pure love; to trust in him; to live upon him; to serve and follow him; and to be perfectly sanctified and made pure, with a divine and heavenly purity. I have, several other times, had views very much of the same nature, and which have had the same effects.[43]

There was nothing in Jonathan Edwards's life that he approached in a superficial manner. He sought knowledge of Scripture and the theological issues of his day with all his intellectual might, but he also understood that his first task as a minister was to cultivate a relational, affectionate, inner knowledge of God. Introverts who follow his lead in combining a relentless, probing intellect with a powerful, personal devotion will radiate both the light and the heat of the gospel.

Mother Teresa, Martin Luther King Jr. and Jonathan Edwards are models to those of us who are called to lead, persuading us not to shy away from our gifts as introverts but to cultivate them and use them for the transformation of the world.

7

Leading as Ourselves

But Moses said to the LORD, "O my Lord, I have never been eloquent,

neither in the past nor even now that you have spoken to your servant;

but I am slow of speech and slow of tongue." Then the LORD said to him,

"Who gives speech to mortals? Who makes them mute or deaf,

seeing or blind? Is it not I, the LORD? Now go, and I will be with your

mouth and teach you what you are to speak." But he said, "O my Lord,

please send someone else."

EXODUS 4:10-13

It is the archetypal story of a reluctant leader. Moses' protests to the unyielding call of God resound every time God's voice summons an unprepared person to an impossible task. Though leaders of all personality types have balked at God's calling, Moses' personality and life exhibit the telltale signs of introversion. In the Hebrew, Exodus 4:10 literally reads "I am not a man of words . . . but I am heavy-tongued and heavy-mouthed." Most introverts can relate to the feeling of our tongues sticking to the floors of mouths, our lips straining to move. We have hesitated and stuttered, not out of torpor but out of the need to think before speaking. Our measured words may come out slowly and deliberately. We have hoped, along with Moses, that God will excuse us from the harrowing task of leadership because of our fears of failure and rejection, because of our nightmare of ineloquence on a public stage.

From the beginning of Moses' story, the narrative theme that stands out is that of *hiding*. Under the cover of two fierce midwives, Moses' mother looked into the eyes of her newborn son and knew she must *hide* him from the bloodthirsty Egyptians. After he became too big to conceal, she made an ark for him and *hid* him among the overgrowth of reeds along the river bank. Discovered, he was raised in the home of the Pharaoh's daughter until, one day, he came across a fellow Hebrew being beaten by an Egyptian. So Moses killed the Egyptian and then *hid* his body in the sand. After Pharaoh heard of this, he aimed to kill Moses, who fled and *hid* in a foreign land. Then, as a shepherd in Midian, Moses drove his flock "beyond the wilderness" (Ex 3:1). I get the sense that Moses was escaping as far away as he possibly could, a warrior turned shepherd, a leader turned alien, an introvert turned refugee. Even when the Lord appeared to him in a blaze of fire, with a voice declaring the transcendent Name, Moses *hid* behind his fears, and then behind the elocution and charisma of his brother, Aaron. Moses went before the Hebrew people and into Pharaoh's throne room clutching his brother's coattails.

As I look at my own leadership experiences and as I talk with introverted pastors, seminarians and those considering leadership in some capacity in the church, I see a similar theme of hiding. We may hide in the shelter of our studies and in the warm embrace of our books, behind our lofty theologies and nuanced understandings of vocation and spirituality. We may conceal our true personalities behind extroverted personas, out of fear of not meeting the expectations of others—or of ourselves. Sometimes we play "the introvert card" in order to avoid taking a risk or doing something uncomfortable.

In my darker moments, I have asked myself whether introverted leaders are capable of surviving the ebb and flow of ministry, with its intensity, risk-taking, relational requirements, and its inevitable moments of weariness, conflict and failure. I have wondered if depression and burnout are unavoidable conditions for those of us who lose energy through interaction. Indeed, Bo, an introverted Korean American woman who had recently left college-campus ministry put this poignant question to me: "Why is it that the thing I love more than anything in the world, being with people, is the very thing that drains me the most?" As much as I cringe when I hear it, there is a reason why some leadership experts call church ministry an extroverted profession.[1] It is draining to meet the social demands of ministry and to constantly battle the expectations of others.

Church leadership is not for every introvert (nor for every extrovert). If you are unwilling to stretch the borders of your personality and your relationships, if you find even one intense social situation to be tiring, or if you are reluctant to speak in most settings, then leadership is likely not for you. As one introverted pastor said to me, "There is no escaping that pastoral ministry is a people business. So pastors must work with people, teach people, counsel people, connect with people. If an introvert cannot or will not step out of his or her internal world in order to be with people, then he or she should probably find another line of work."

However, in more than a decade of Christian leadership I have come to see the significant contributions introverts make to others and have learned effective introverted models of leadership. So we must distinguish between our energy level for a task and our gifting for that same task. Just because we lose energy doing something does not necessarily indicate we are not a good fit for it. I am convinced that calling, not personality type, is the determinative factor in the formation and longevity of a leader. It was no coincidence that God met Moses in the very place that he tried to flee, nor was it accidental that Moses would later drive another flock, the people of Israel, into that same wilderness to the mountain of God. God's call sheds light on our darkest hiding places.

What stands out to me about my conversations with introverted pastors is their firm conviction that they labor in the power of God. They did not necessarily choose church ministry because they found a perfect match for their gifts or personality type. My friend Chris said, in spite of the fact he was operating out of weaknesses much of the time, "I still believe God has called me to pastoral ministry. I have had to conclude that God may call some people into work for which they are not perfectly suited, for his greater glory." Another pastor said, "I'm not a very charismatic person, but I refuse to use that as an excuse not to do something. The power of the Holy Spirit gives us the ability to do things we couldn't do otherwise. If I absolutely need to be a charismatic leader for two hours to accomplish something, I think God has the ability to do that."

When Moses objected to God at the burning bush, saying that he was a clumsy speaker, God did not disagree with him. The Lord did not say, "Not true, Moses, I've heard you speak and you inspired me! You're going places as a preacher!" He said "I will be with your mouth and teach you what you are to speak" (Ex 4:12). *I will be with you. I will give you the words.* These are the bedrock reassurances that God offers to those he calls to lead. Our leadership credentials are the wisdom and the Spirit of the Lord. God doesn't promise that leadership will be easy or always natural. God promises that his presence will go with those that he calls, and in his presence is a power that transcends all human abilities. More than a millennium after Moses, God put it to the apostle Paul this way: "My grace is sufficient for you, for power is made perfect in weakness" (2 Cor 12:9). Paul would then be able to say "It is no longer I who live, but it is Christ who lives in me" (Gal 2:20). It is out of God's power, not self-power, that leaders minister to others.

Amidst ravaging supernatural plagues and pyrotechnics of burning bushes and smoldering mountains, I think that the most dramatic moment in the story of Moses centers around a shift in pronouns. Throughout the story of Moses' call, the exodus and the handing down of the law, Moses persisted in referring to the Hebrews as "your people," God's possession. He was distancing himself from his kinsfolk. But in Exodus 34, God showed Moses his glory, passing by him in an unprecedented theophany while Moses hid in a crevice of the mountain, his eyes sheltered from the fullness of God's majestic holiness. Moses then prayed to the Lord: "If now I have found favor in your sight, O Lord, I pray, let the Lord go with us. Although this is a stiff-necked people, pardon our iniquity and our sin, and take us for your inheritance" (Ex 34:9). Go with *us*. Pardon *our* iniquity and *our* sin, and take *us* for your inheritance. Moses finally came out of hiding; he claimed his people, his true heritage and identity.

Moses' transformation demonstrates that a deep, intimate relationship with God is not exclusive of a profound love for people. Indeed, when we behold the glory of the Lord, we claim his people as our own.

THRIVING IN MINISTRY

Calling belongs to God, and it is the foundational reason why introverts venture into Christian leadership. A sense of vocation is what sustains us, and though we do not determine our vocation, we can learn how to protect it and to thrive in it through self-care, spiritual disciplines, thoughtfulness about how we expend our energy, and a healthy perspective on our role in the ministry of the church.

Self-care. Perhaps the most vital ingredient to longevity in ministry for a leader is self-care. We devote so much time and energy to caring for the spiritual and emotional needs of others that we can neglect our own needs—both to our detriment and to the long-term detriment of those that we care for. The less we pay attention to ourselves, the less we have to offer others over the long term.

Many introverted pastors confess that the hardest part of their job is dealing with the disappointment of others, the inevitable result of unmet expectations. This has been most distressing when people have expressed dissatisfaction in their leadership abilities. Facing the disappointment of others seems to take a greater toll on introverts because we habitually internalize everything and can be conflict avoidant. One introverted pastor lamented how personally he took criticism, always shamefully asking "What did I do wrong" first, before even considering that others might have been in error as well.

Roy Oswald and Otto Kroeger reflect on the struggles of introverted leaders as they analyze the leadership of Moses: "Throughout his ministry Moses is continually exasperated with the children of Israel. Their moaning, groaning, whimpering drive him crazy. So great is his frustration and anger that he takes it to God: 'Am I a mother that I need to coddle these people through the wilderness?' Later in his ministry we hear him pray, 'God, if you are at all merciful, let me die here on the spot. Do not let me view my own misery any longer.' "[2] Moses allowed the complaints of others to fester in his soul, eating away like acid at his sense of call and joy in serving God.

There is a psychological term for a condition that people who work in caring professions develop: *compassion fatigue.* It often assumes one of two forms, though in the most debilitating cases, caregivers are stricken with both: depression, as the sadness of others infects them, or callousness to the pain of others out of self-protection. I was a hospice chaplain for seventeen months, and in that time, I counted six bouts of compassion fatigue. I confess that at the end of some weeks, after caring and praying for terminally ill patients, claiming for them the gentle presence of God and the hope of resurrection, I came home and felt nothing but emptiness and resentment. All I wanted was to hide in my private sanctuary, sheltered from the needs and the urgency of other people.

Self-care must move in both an *internal* and *external* direction. *Internally,* introverted leaders must seek wholeness in their spiritual and emotional lives. Mother Teresa counseled her missionary sisters that "the interior must become the main power of the exterior."[3] We need to cultivate our practice of spiritual disciplines, which for many introverts is a natural strength. In spiritual disciplines, such as prayer, writing, biblical meditation and fasting, we consciously place ourselves in the presence of God. Because introverts ponder the complexity of our internal lives, we battle the voices in our heads that would push us toward hopelessness and prevent us from acting in faith, but spiritual disciplines open us to the voice of God, which brings comfort and restoration to our souls. For introverted leaders to be healthy, God's voice of grace and love needs to drown out the voices of self-doubt and failure. We need to have the proper gauge for success in leadership, which is always faithfulness to our calling. Spiritual disciplines are arenas for God's voice to battle with the other voices.

Many introverted pastors regularly take personal retreats. Extroverts might find the notion of extended solitude maddening, but for introverts retreats are a time of rediscovering God and redefining ourselves. My colleague said that when she goes on a silent retreat, it takes twenty-four hours for the running thoughts in her head to dissipate. Another pastor would take a weeklong retreat every August at a nearby monastery in order to prepare spiritually for the fall and to start the exegetical work on his next sermon series. A missionary friend of mine regularly takes four-day retreats to a Catholic abbey in the California desert, where she participates in their practice of the divine hours. She finds it easier to connect with God through silence, art and ritual than through the chatty fellowship and unstructured worship of her church.

Our self-care must also move in an *outward* direction. There have been too many examples of Christian leaders who have been ensnared in soul-destroying, career-ending temptation for us to ignore the importance of this. Archibald Hart, in his classic book on clergy depression, observed that

> The loneliness of ministry . . . can shape the minister toward being cut off from support systems. It can keep him from having close confidants with whom problems of the work can be discussed. It is a psychological fact that one cannot resolve conflicts or clarify issues simply by thinking about them. Self-talk and introspective rumination with no outside input leads inevitably to distortion and irrationality, whereas talking things over with someone else can help to clarify issues, and remove distortions. Every minister needs close confidants—staff, family, other ministers, trusted laypersons in the congregation—to help in this clarifying process.[4]

Hart's observation that introspection without any other influence leads to distortion is especially penetrating for introverted leaders. Even though our internal process is incredibly valuable, there is clarity that comes from speaking out loud. God never intended for even the most introverted person to live life without reference to others. Isolation is never an indicator of spiritual health. As introverted leaders, we need to surround ourselves with a small group of trusted people who are able to shed light on our blind spots and receive us without judgment. It's in being embraced as we are that we find the courage to face what is truly going on inside of us.

There are many places where we can find the support that we need. Many introverted ministers enjoy relationships with introverted colleagues. People with shared experiences help normalize our experiences as introverts, and in simply trading stories and struggles, we find greater self-acceptance and strength. The therapy setting is also a valuable setting for introverted leaders. The one-on-one environment is a natural fit, and I have found that in therapy I am put in a situation where I, a habitual listener, am forced to speak about myself. The confidentiality and professional trust in the therapeutic setting enables me to open up the layers of my life that I don't generally show others. Given that introverts are prone to burnout faster than their extroverted counterparts, I would even say that regular therapy, spiritual direction or some form of relationship with a trusted counselor should be mandatory for introverted pastors.

One concern that introverted pastors regularly express about their lives in ministry is striking a balance between professional life and family life. This tension is a concern for pastors of all temperamental profiles, but the introverted slant is finding energy for our families after spending our days caring for others. While an extrovert may occasionally come from work energized, introverts are invariably weary. One pastor lamented that "after a day of meeting with people in pain, all I want to do when I get home is crawl inside of myself, but I have a husband and two kids there who want, and deserve, my attention." She and her husband, an extrovert, process stress differently. She internalizes things and usually works through them on her own, whereas he manages stress by talking it through with her. Conflict ensues when she does not have the energy to listen or when he considers her to be withholding from him.

Scheduling. Mature introverted leaders have learned how to monitor their energy levels and are experts in knowing how to save and restore their energy. Therefore, if introverts want endurance and joy in ministry, and in their personal lives, we must be thoughtful about scheduling. Those who prefer high degrees of flexibility and spontaneity may resist this suggestion, but I am unable to avoid the conclusion that careful planning is a central factor in preventing burnout and compassion fatigue.[5]

When I was a hospice chaplain, I learned to space out my appointments with patients so that I would have recovery time between meetings. I also took an hour lunch every day, unless called away for an emergency. In the late afternoon, I would carve out time for solitude, so that I could recharge before my wife came home from work. Other introverts find that short naps or other ways of storing up energy before a socially draining event help them weather the rhythms of ministry. From a weekly outlook, I would fit my patient visits into four days, so that on the fifth day I could document my visits and make phone calls from home. My wife and I also agreed that one night a week would be "introvert night" so that I could use the evening however I chose. On a larger scale, I needed to take at least one vacation day every four weeks, and a whole week every three months, which was right about the time compassion fatigue would set in. Most importantly, I had to learn how to decline even appealing invitations when they interfered with my rhythms of self-care. To an introverted leader, the magic word may not be "please," it may be "no." I know an introverted pastor and sought-out conference speaker who, during busy months, will preschedule "NOTHING" days into his calendar, a few days per month when he bans himself from any events or meetings. He shares his calendar with a few trusted friends who hold him accountable to leave those days open.

However, even as we are intentional about our scheduling, we must leave room for the surprising work of God. Henri Nouwen once had a conversation with a Notre Dame professor, who marveled to him: "You know . . . my whole life I have been complaining that my work was constantly interrupted, until I discovered that interruptions were my work."[6] Introverts can become so absorbed in our internal worlds that we miss the needs of others around us. Our scheduling and emotional boundaries must not preempt the divine interjections that shape so much of our identity and our work. We must remember that the events that form the foundation of our calling—the incarnation of the Son of God and his resurrection from the dead—were cosmic interruptions in a world that had grown callous to God's movements.

DIRECTING PEOPLE TOWARD GOD

Preaching. Those who are only aware of the stereotypes of introverted behavior—shy, awkward, reticent, timid—might assume that introverts will be public speaking disasters. When I was a seminary student, I interned at a Presbyterian church where I shared an office with a cantankerous Irish woman. After hearing that I would be preaching on a Sunday morning, she remarked in her thick brogue to the receptionist: "How could Adam possibly preach in church? He never talks!" Yet the exhilaration of preaching that Sunday morning, along with the encouragement of the congregation, set me on a path of preaching and teaching that I intend to follow for the rest of my life.

One of the most unexpected findings of my research was that introverted pastors felt very comfortable preaching, irrespective of congregation size. Many of them actually considered it their biggest strength and favorite part of the job. They found that their natural tendencies toward study, scholarship and writing translated into effective preaching and teaching. My colleague Cynthia said that, for her, preaching is the *easiest* part of ministry. Some introverted pastors find preaching less challenging than the unstructured nature of the fellowship hour after the service, where the sturdiest Styrofoam cups can't hide their rapidly depleting energy. A member of a 1,500-member congregation remarked that his introverted pastor was "bipolar": energetic and affable in the pulpit, wilting and awkward afterward.

Introverts often feel confident preaching because it is in a controlled setting. Preaching moves in a unilateral direction, from speaker to listener. The person up front sets the goal and the tone, and has the luxury of speaking without interruption. Uninterrupted speaking is generally more comfortable for introverts than dialogue, because the give and take of the latter requires us to think on our feet. Introverts prefer to prepare thoroughly in advance, and settings like debates or question-and-answer sessions can devolve into rambling presentations or what my friend Mark calls a "Festival of Umm."

We need to take into account our personality preferences and strengths when we consider our strategies for sermon preparation and delivery. I have found that my preaching is best when I have written out a full manuscript of my sermon beforehand, because I find Marti Olsen Laney's claim that introverts have a slower mechanism for "word retrieval"[7] to be true when I am speaking in public. My diction is not of the same quality and fluidity when I have not written my sermons out in advance. Because I love to craft words and sentences and I appreciate the impact that language can have on people, I often enjoy the writing and preparation components of preaching more than I do the act of preaching.

The challenge for me, and others who pen full sermons, is translating the written manuscript into an engaging interaction in the pulpit. Some of us empathize with the apostle Paul, whose accusers contended that "his letters are weighty and strong, but his bodily presence is weak, and his speech contemptible" (2 Cor 10:10). We write with a flourish, but we speak with a thud. If we, as many of the introverted pastors I spoke with do, bring a full text (or a thorough outline) with us to the pulpit, we may become bound to the world of our manuscripts, preaching *at* people rather than communicating *with* them. Our sermons may seem overly rhetorical because they are unintentionally written for people to read rather than to hear. When this happens, we neglect the primary relational component in preaching, as preaching is a relationship-building opportunity.

Whereas some extroverted preachers may struggle with repetitiveness and superficiality, some introverted preachers may err on the side of erudition or ambiguity. Our ideas may be profound but they may not settle in the actual, tangible lives of our listeners. With all of these potential hazards, I emphasize the following things when I mentor young introverted preachers:

1. Preach as an introvert, not an extrovert. Use thoughtful pauses and silence as a way to add gravity and contemplativeness to your sermons.

2. Modulate your voice. People hear the tone of your voice before they hear your words. You will hold their attention better by changing the pitch and tone of your voice, and a significant component of persuasion is the conviction with which you share your ideas.

3. Break up your lofty ideas and biblical exposition with stories, examples and illustrations. They help put flesh on your ideas and makes them tangible to people.

4. Preach to inspire, not merely inform (suggestions three and four are particularly important for introverts who score high in the thinking category of MBTI).

5. Be present. Introverts are prone to get caught up in their sermon notes and their presentation, giving the impression that they are not fully present to the congregation.

6. Don't show your homework. Be thorough in your study and preparation, but in the actual sermon, keep your research and thinking process in the background.

7. Don't be intimidated by mistakes. If you stumble over your words or lose your place, people may actually feel more connected with you and listen more carefully.

8. Use preaching as an opportunity for self-revelation.

This last point has been somewhat controversial, but for me, there has been no better arena to share more of myself and to connect with others. In other settings, I listen more than I talk and am disinclined toward talking about myself. I think introverted preachers should take advantage of a preaching opportunity to introduce deeper layers of themselves to others. Some contend that preaching should only be about biblical exposition, but even in that, we are giving people our perspective on Scripture and the world. If we are offering our worldviews to people, then why not also present them with other aspects of ourselves—our hearts, our weaknesses, our questions?

A groundbreaking, and somewhat unsettling, discovery for me was that congregations evaluate the quality of preaching not by the profundity of a person's ideas but by their level of trust in the preacher as a person. A recent study on preaching found that the credibility of a preacher is first a function of the *relationships* they have with their listeners. This study found that "where that relationship was positive and when laity perceived that the preacher had genuine concern for them (i.e., displaying openness and warmth, exercising and dealing kindly and seriously with their opinions), hearers assumed the Word of God was being preached."[8] The relational packaging overshadows, though also confirms, the content. Thus even the most insightful biblical interpretation and robust theological reflections can fall flat if people do not trust the speaker. This explains why sometimes, when I have preached to unfamiliar congregations, I have felt like the court jester performing for an audience that just pushed away from Thanksgiving dinner. But other times, when preaching to people whose homes I have been in, I've felt like I could read the phone book and people would melt into tears and speak in tongues.

We introverts, so often captivated by ideas, need to take seriously that Marshall McLuhan's immortal line, "the medium is the message," goes beyond the field of advertising. For preaching, *we* are the medium. The message resides in us as persons.[9] The most pivotal preaching event in the Bible was not Moses and the Ten

Commandments at Mount Sinai, or Peter on Pentecost, or even the Sermon on the Mount; the most pivotal preaching moment was the incarnation, the moment the eternal Word of God, the wisdom with which the whole universe hangs together, became human. God's supreme revelatory medium was not words piped in or scrolls dropped from the heavens, but a living, breathing human being who walked and taught and ate and wept and loved among us.[10]

I have come to realize that, though I have gifts rooted in words (in quality, not quantity), I simply cannot be an effective communicator unless I build others' trust. The way that I develop others' trust is to lead by example and to invest personally in others' lives, which means I need to come down from my ivory tower and involve myself in the details of their everyday existence. As an introverted pastor, I feel that I am skilled in the "big" communication events—preaching and teaching, casting vision, leading meetings —but I struggle with "small" communication—small talk, saying the little things that make people feel known and appreciated, expressing interest in the details of people's lives, or even returning phone calls promptly. Yet if we are to preach that God is not only involved in the big matters of salvation, redemption and justice, but is also in the routine circumstances of daily life, then we leaders need to show an interest in the ordinary events of people's lives. People will watch what we do before they listen to what we say.

Sharing your life. The biblical passage that has become foundational for both my leadership and my preaching is Paul's tender word to the believers in Thessalonica: "So deeply do we care for you that we were determined to share with you not only the gospel of God but also our own selves, because you have become very dear to us" (1 Thess 2:8). What stands out to me here is, first, the deep affection that Paul had for the Thessalonian believers. His motivation for communicating the gospel, as emphasized twice in one short verse, is his care and love for them.

But it's even more striking that Paul was committed to not only sharing the gospel, the content of the faith, but also his own life. He loved them so much that he shared more than the message of Jesus; he shared himself. The nature of the gospel is such that it can only be fully imparted through shared life and authentic personal relationships.

Christian leaders, even introverted ones, are called to enter into the worlds of others and allow others to enter ours. We let others see our strengths and our triumphs, as well as our weaknesses and failures and doubts, even our struggles as introverts (using discretion, of course). The greatest gift that we have to offer others is ourselves, because it's in our fragile and vulnerable humanness that people see the unconditional love and redeeming power of God most clearly. A leader showing vulnerability about his or her personal life, thus creating empathy with the pain and struggles of others, often has a greater impact than countless numbers of the most powerful biblical exhortations. I've found this to be especially true when I tell unresolved personal stories, meaning that the story hasn't ended in victory and personal heroism; this presents me as a fellow traveler in the way of the cross.

Leading out loud. Even though introverts are bent toward listening and reflection, introverts called into positions of leadership in Christian communities, especially in evangelical communities, will do much of our leading by speaking or writing. What this requires is a deliberate effort on our part to translate our reflections and inner processes into words. If we are convinced that introverts can be effective leaders, and that we bring different gifts to the table than extroverts, we will benefit others by verbalizing and modeling the strengths we have.

We know that introspection is valuable for leaders, not only for personal growth but also for bringing transformation to the organizations they lead, but I would argue that our culture is becoming increasingly deaf to the internal voices that indicate to us that something is wrong. We have become alarmingly dependent on the external voices—advertising, mass appeal, technology—as the basis for our choices and actions. When I was a pastor in a church in Southern California, I was troubled by how few people reflected on the ways they spent their day-to-day lives and how few of them considered what their choices communicate about their priorities. In fact, to many of them, it seemed like the element of "choice" was absent. It was as though there were inexorable external forces that constrained them to lead the lives they did, as if they were mere victims of cultural drivenness, the hectic ambition of quiet suburban life. I wondered why people were afraid to slow down and what they would discover if they took the time to listen to their internal voices.

People in our culture need models of self-reflection, leaders who will teach them how to look inward and evaluate their motivations and choices. Introverted leaders should look to model that in pastoral interactions, in meetings, in preaching, in newsletters and e-mails, even casually or humorously in social situations. As Henri Nouwen said, "Our task is the opposite of distraction. Our task is to help people concentrate on the real but often hidden event of God's active presence in their lives. Hence the question that must guide all organizing activity in a parish is not how to keep people busy but how to keep them from being so busy that they can no longer hear the voice of God who speaks into the silence."[11]

Spiritual direction. Spiritual direction is an ancient practice in which people collaborate to practice listening to God. Ordinarily, it involves a one-on-one setting in which there is a spiritual director and a spiritual directee, though it can also involve larger groups. The practice of spiritual direction is founded on the notion that we are never the ones who initiate the conversation; God is already speaking and moving among us, as the Spirit hovered over the waters in Genesis 1, and our role is to discern and respond. A spiritual director helps the directee attend to the voice of the Spirit. Jeannette Bakke explains that "Present-day directors do not give answers or tell directees what to do in their relationship with God or when making life choices. Instead, they listen with directees for how the Spirit of God is present and active. Directors support and encourage directees as they listen and respond to God."[12]

As I have participated in spiritual direction, both from the standpoint of a director and directee, I have become convinced that this ministry is tailor-made for introverts. The majority of my classmates in my spiritual-direction-training program were introverts. For introverted leaders who constantly feel like they are operating out of their weaknesses, spiritual direction plays to our strengths:

1. The setting is one-on-one, perhaps the most comfortable introverted context.

2. The relationship is ongoing, sometimes enduring over years, and involves mutual commitment. This fosters depth of relationship and enables people to explore the spiritual life thoroughly. Introverts are much better over time.

3. The primary role of the spiritual director is listening, not speaking. A good spiritual director is comfortable with silence and knows how to ask probing questions. She also understands that excessive advice and instruction can short-circuit the path to wisdom and maturity for another person.

4. Spiritual directors must be able to detect nuance and listen for what's unsaid. They are listening to three separate frequencies simultaneously: the wavelength of the Spirit, the experiences and thoughts of the directee, and the movements in themselves.

5. A director is a kind of spiritual observer, who removes herself enough to "watch" what God is doing in the life of another person and then reports on what she sees.

I wish to commend not only the particular niche of spiritual direction to introverted leaders but also the general habits exercised in spiritual direction, which I think can be applied fruitfully in all pastoral settings. My friend Scott, an introverted pastor who works with a missionary organization, says that he thinks of himself as a "contemplative presence." In whatever setting he is in, he tries not only to listen to the overtones of what people are saying but also to listen to the undercurrents. He asks himself questions, *What are the emotions and the assumptions behind what people are saying? What is the Holy Spirit saying? What is happening inside myself?* If he "hears" something that seems significant, he will speak up in an appropriate moment. This is a discipline he particularly tries to apply in planning meetings, because he knows the tendency in spiritual communities to lapse into business agendas while neglecting to listen.

In my interactions with pastors over the past decade, I have been confounded by how few of them were adept in the discipline of listening. What should be an absolute prerequisite for entering ministry has been subordinated to the all important evangelical qualities of speech—teaching, persuasion, correction—or relegated to specific "side" ministries. Our seminaries subject hopeful pastors to rigorous communication and preaching classes, but I have never seen a class or seminar offered on listening.

Jesus had a piercing listening ability. He practiced the sort of listening that could undress people, exposing their motivations, weaknesses, longings and hopes. In John 4, in his famously scandalous conversation with the Samaritan woman at the well of Jacob, Jesus not only paid attention to the words in their conversation but he listened for the echoes of her deepest fears and longings underneath her words. She talked about wells and water, but he perceived the cavernous well in her soul that she tried to fill with unsatisfying relationships. He listened for what was unsaid. And then, with one devastating request, that she go and return with her "husband," Jesus shattered her walls and opened her up to the soul-quenching water of life.

Many people speak about suffering and pain in a circumspect manner. Out of self-protection, they may speak of emotions such as "hurt" or "despair" in a rational way. Or they may spiritualize their circumstances and feelings, framing their pain as a theological issue or question. It's often very ineffective to respond to people according to these methods of expression, because the true issues are often unspoken. Many introverts, who are versed in the workings of the inner world, are naturally equipped for the art of listening to what's unsaid.

I remember when a female college student asked me, in the presence of a group of students, "Adam, how do you know if you are a Christian?" I let the other students chime in for a while. They cited Scripture, talked about experiences, gave theological reasoning and talked about faith as the opposite of evidence. I could tell the woman was getting angrier and angrier as they spoke. While they were responding, I tried to listen to what was underneath her question. After a while, I said, "What I hear you saying is that you feel really alone and unloved." Tears immediately streamed down her face. She opened up about her life and her fears and her sense of inadequacy. We then had the chance to surround her and pray for her, and she left feeling a little more loved, a little less alone, a little closer to God.

This pattern of asking for one thing but actually wanting something else also takes place on a corporate level. For example, even though people in congregations may verbalize that they want leaders who can swell the membership and the budget of their churches, the wise leaders among the congregation will know sometimes to look underneath those measurements. Many people are reluctant to express their deepest longings and hopes, so they project them into superficial, quantifiable gauges that give the appearance of success and vitality. They subconsciously hope that achieving those goals will bring healing and joy to their souls, which of course it never will. They might say they want church growth, but sometimes what they actually need is something much more profound and personal. Perhaps they may need to know that God's grace is big enough to reach them in the wilderness, or that he is present in the most vulnerable and dark places of their lives. The best leaders know to, sometimes, not give people what they ask for.

The ministry of presence. Another gift that introverted leaders exercise is the ministry of presence. Too often people think that if someone is in pain, they need to solve that person's problems, to "fix it." They think they need to lift him or her out of anguish, and wish they could handle the situation like an ER doctor: sweep in, diagnose the problem, defibrillate, start the IV, move on. But I'm convinced that a person who is suffering does not, primarily, need answers or a well-timed statement that sheds light on the situation. Because when people try to impart their "wisdom" into a person's struggle, it can have a polarizing effect: they reveal how little they know the situation, and the person feels even more isolated. Few things intensify a person's pain as much as glib answers or nervous chatter from people who are uncomfortable with silence.

What a person in pain needs, on the deepest human level, is to not feel alone. What helps someone is people who will simply be there and help carry the burden without always trying to fix the situation. The best thing Job's "comforters" ever did was sit with him on the ground in silence for seven days. I'm sure he wished that on the eighth day they had just returned home, without ever opening their mouths. Words can trivialize, but silence is sacred.

WHAT INTROVERTED LEADERSHIP LOOKS LIKE

One of the things I've accepted is that I will impact fewer people than extroverted pastors. At times I have compared myself negatively with my extroverted counterparts who have more widespread influence. But I have come to see this "limitation" as an opportunity to have a deeper impact on the people I do influence.

Extroverts can err on the side of scattering themselves too widely and only impacting people superficially. As an introvert, I find it far more satisfying to invest in a few people, and I trust that my intentional efforts will result in mature disciples and leaders who will go on to further impact the church and the world.

Biblical scholars have observed that, though Jesus scattered gospel seeds far and wide, he devoted the bulk of his ministry, especially in the Gospel of Mark, to cultivating the spiritual lives and the understanding of the twelve disciples. He narrowed this focus even further, investing more deeply in the development of the three: Peter, James and John. These were the ones he gave nicknames, and they were the only disciples privileged to witness his transfiguration (Mk 9:2-4), the resurrection of Jairus's daughter (Mk 5:22-24, 35-43) and his anguish in the garden of Gethsemane (Mk 14:32-41). Jesus, as he consciously moved toward his fate, established successors who would anchor his kingdom mission to the ends of the earth. He taught them, corrected them, modeled both faith and struggle for them, and exposed them to unsettling and stretching experiences.

Even though introverted leaders have learned, out of a mixture of necessity and guilt, how to cater to the masses, we innately desire to invest in "the few." Intimate, ongoing relationships—in which we enter deeply into the lives of others and impart wisdom —are our modus operandi. In my ministry, my greatest satisfaction has come through the relationships I've been involved in via spiritual direction, mentoring or ongoing counseling relationships. In these ministries, I am able to help people discover their gifts and discern God's direction for their lives; I can utilize my natural capacities for listening and understanding nuance. These relationships are energizing and full of joy, and they are strategic in passing on what I have learned to people who will then do the same for others.

I have seen the strategy of concentrating on "the few" applied very effectively in youth ministry, a sector of church ministry where extroverted leadership has been especially idealized. In my research, I came across myriads of youth-minister job descriptions that echoed this one: "The ideal candidate will have a dynamic personality and be energized by people, as well as the ability to invest in relationships outside of the office." Translation: Only extroverted applications accepted. Popular thinking is that youth are attracted to "the show," a glitzy program with high production value and a zany, uber-charismatic youth pastor.

But I would argue that, though the cult of personality woos, personal attention is what truly impacts. Due to the state of the American family, youth workers often function as surrogate parents. Given the choice, would you want a parent who is up front entertaining all your friends or would you want a parent who will remember your birthday? When I was a college pastor, the students who came onto campus with the greatest maturity, spiritual depth and understanding of the gospel were invariably those who'd had a youth pastor or other mentor from their communities of faith take a special, personal interest in them. Moreover, many of those students had been the beneficiaries of a movement toward contemplative youth ministry, in which the primary role of youth pastors is less about creating entertaining programs and more about helping students cultivate an awareness of God's presence.[13] Contemplative youth ministry is a promising new direction both for introverted youth workers and for the introverted students they lead.

Equipping. When Jethro, Moses' father-in-law, ventured into the desert to discover what the Lord had done among the people of Israel, he was troubled to find Moses at the center of a maelstrom of people seeking instruction and mediation. His advice to Moses is shrewd:

What you are doing is not good. You will surely wear yourself out, both you and these people with you. For the task is too heavy for you; you cannot do it alone. Now listen to me. I will give you counsel, and God be with you! You should represent the people before God, and you should bring their cases before God; teach them the statutes and instructions and make known to them the way they are to go and the things they are to do. You should also look for able men among all the people, men who fear God, are trustworthy, and hate dishonest gain; set such men over them as officers over thousands, hundreds, fifties and tens. Let them sit as judges for the people at all times; let them bring every important case to you, but decide every minor case themselves. So it will be easier for you, and they will bear the burden with you. If you do this, and God so commands you, then you will be able to endure, and all these people will go to their home in peace. (Ex 18:17-23)

The introverted pastors I interviewed were insistent that their roles are not to be the ministry providers, with everyone else positioned as ministry recipients, but their roles are to equip others to do the ministry of the church. Most of them pointed to Ephesians 4:11-13 as the basis of their self-understanding:

The gifts he gave were that some would be apostles, some prophets, some evangelists, some pastors and teachers, to equip the saints for the work of ministry, for building up the body of Christ, until all of us come to the unity of the faith and of the knowledge of the Son of God, to maturity, to the measure of the full stature of Christ.

These three verses are packed with insight about leadership. We see that God creates different sorts of leaders and that they, therefore, lead out of who they are and the gifts they have been given. We also learn that the main responsibility of leaders, with their manifold gifts and functions, is to equip others for ministry and pave the way for their maturity. In order for pastors to be faithful to their biblical calling, and survive in ministry, they must empower and release others to also do the ministry of the church.

My friend Chris, an introverted Presbyterian pastor in the northeastern United States, has been wrestling with the implications of the biblical emphasis on equipping: "As a solo pastor, I must find the right people and then give them the power to do those other functions. That does not mean *helping me* to do those functions. It means that *they* do those tasks, and I contribute how I can. It also means developing and educating a congregation that allows laypeople to lead in ways previously reserved for and expected of the pastor."

Chris concedes that he, like many introverts, is not naturally a team builder. George Barna lists team building as one of the four leadership aptitudes that comprise the "ideal" leadership team. The most challenging part of team building for introverts is not making the necessary personal connections with others, but it's facilitating the connections that must take place *between* other people in the community. This facilitation requires someone who is capable of gathering people into social situations that will form cohesive communities, and the truth is that this usually requires a socially tireless extrovert who thrives in group situations. However, the refreshing news is that, when you have a team-leadership model, an introverted pastor does not have to play that role. The introverted pastor can, instead, encourage and equip others to assume the team-building functions, and he or she can focus on other critical areas that contribute to the vitality and reach of the community.

Team leadership. The prophet Micah reviews God's favor to Israel at the time of the exodus: "For I brought you up from the land of Egypt, / and redeemed you from the house of slavery; / and I sent before you Moses, Aaron, and Miriam" (Mic 6:4). Even Moses, the most celebrated Old Testament leader, led in the context of a team of people. Aaron was the spokesman, Moses' mouthpiece, and Miriam was the worship leader, the one who led the Hebrews in triumphant verse after their liberation. Together the three oversaw the transition from an enslaved people ruled by an oppressor to an independent nation governed by the gracious law of the Lord.

From the trio of leaders in the exodus to the tribal heads of the burgeoning nation of Israel, to the apostolic community appointed by Jesus to continue his kingdom mission, to Paul's intimate partnerships in his Gentile ministry, team leadership is a mainstay in biblical tradition. It's not the only form of biblical leadership— thinking of the rugged isolation of the Old Testament prophets— but it is the one that I most recommend to introverted leaders. The lonely-at-the-top model of leadership, which may be a temptation for many introverted leaders, is increasingly irrelevant in a postmodern culture; it is spiritually dangerous for leaders and a less effective use of our resources and energy.

Postmodernity has precipitated shifts in our leadership paradigms. In modernity, a hierarchical model of leadership was normative, and people separated themselves from others through expertise and position. Postmodern culture facilitates more egalitarian and collaborative forms of leadership and ministry. A successful postmodern leader will motivate others through relational skills and persuasion, not position and decree. Leadership in postmodern culture is not appointed by the Powers-That-Be; true leadership is *given* by a community to those people who have earned their trust and respect. Thus, in this culture, introverts must battle our tendency to lead from a position above others, simply giving commands and directions from a distance because it requires less social energy.

Team leadership reduces the pressure placed on the individual leader and helps ameliorate the sense of loneliness "at the top," which especially afflicts introverts. Though corporate CEOs and megachurch pastors often seemed resigned to this fate, I am convinced that this isolation does not have to be, and should not be, the case. There have been far too many scandals in the evangelical world for us to continue to place leaders in situations of considerable pressure and limited accountability. Even in stain-glassed cathedrals, power corrupts. Leading in teams helps reduce the glare of the spotlight on one person and distributes responsibility.

The team-leadership model recognizes that the traditional model of leadership, in which "pastors lead everyone and must have direct, unfettered oversight of the masses,"[14] asks pastors to be superhuman, meeting the needs of everyone in the community, in all their diversity. In a team setting, leadership is shared by a community of people, which counters the tendency for pastors to form congregations in their own images. George Barna describes the shift to leading in a team setting: "In a team environment, the leadership role of the pastor shifts from that of leading the entire congregation to being a leader of leaders. . . . This team-leadership model reduces the stress on the pastor from having to be all things to all people and essentially becoming nothing to everyone. The pastor may instead pour whatever he or she has into the relative handful of fellow leaders, who in turn provide the breadth and the depth of leadership that the church requires."[15]

Team leadership enables introverted leaders to focus and to devote more time to their passions and giftings, which is life-giving. Though our primary source of energy will come through solitude, introverts can also find energy in a job that fits our spiritual gifts and interests. Nothing taxes introverts' energy faster than job requirements that do not match who we are. Though I gained a great deal from my years as a hospice chaplain, spending the bulk of my time with people in crisis and then thoroughly documenting those visits was not where I wanted to be. I longed to be a teacher and spiritual director and writer, and it's in those pursuits that I have found life and energy.

Partnerships between introverts and extroverts. I consider a partnership between introverted and extroverted leaders—both professional and lay—to be imperative in leading the church. Their complementary strengths bring vitality and wholeness to ministry, and they model faithfulness for both introverts and extroverts in the community. I cannot overstate how validating and transformative it is for individuals in a community to see people who share their personality type leading out of who they are.

My most effective partnership with an extrovert developed in college campus ministry. I say "developed" because it did not come easily or naturally. Jonny was the team leader, with the experience and expertise in college ministry, and I was the new staff member, equipped with a seminary education and a background in preaching and hospital chaplaincy. Jonny was the most extroverted person I had ever met, one of those people that can carry on a conversation with anyone, about anything. He has gifts in evangelism and community building, and people would flock to him like paparazzi to an A-list celebrity. If I didn't know it to be physiologically impossible, I would have thought Jonny could have forgone sleep to have his REM cycles powered by social interaction. I, on the other hand, am highly introverted, a deep thinker, with gifts in teaching and pastoring. He thought I spent too little time with people and too much time in study and preparation, and I was constantly consoling people who wondered why he was always spending time with *other* people in the community.

We spent several months trying to understand each other, having to forgive each other and endure the requisite growing pains of two very different people trying to lead the same community. Yet after a while, we developed a synergy that transcended our own individual contributions. I created a cohesive vision for the direction of the community, and he, with his finger on the pulse of the community, fostered camaraderie and enthusiasm. I mentored introverted leaders that he might have overlooked, and he discipled extroverted leaders who were drawn to his energy. Likewise our preaching styles balanced each other as well: a graduate later told me that when Jonny preached, it felt like he preached to the whole community, and when I preached, it felt like I preached to each individual in the community. I gave them probing ideas to chew on, and he communicated a passion for relationships.

Finding your place. In that partnership, in which I was not the principal leader, I learned that I prefer a leadership position that is a step removed from the center of a community. Though I am a competent administrator and team leader, I find that I enjoy being a shade away from the limelight, as I have greater freedom to determine my own schedule. When I have been the head of a community, I found that I was too often at the whims and schedules of others, and I spent more time reacting than I did initiating. When I'm on the side, I am able to devote more time to what I love, like writing, studying and teaching, and I am able to move at a more leisurely pace.

My friend Charles agrees that, while he enjoys making contributions to teams, he does not like the role of central leader. He interprets his ministry in light of the biblical character Barnabas, who came alongside others and raised them up to be leaders, while he remained in the background. Barnabas, who earned the honorific title "son of encouragement," was given the harrowing task of mentoring fire-breathing-Saul after his conversion on the Damascus road. The first stories in which we see the two of them together, they are listed as "Barnabas and Saul," but then in Acts 13:42 the order is reversed to "Paul and Barnabas," a pattern that endures throughout the book. In Greek narrative, the person listed first is the most prominent person. Barnabas had done his role of preparing Paul to be the head of the mission to the Gentiles, and had, without jealousy or resentment, taken second place behind him.

Other introverted leaders, however, find the opposite to be true.

My friend Karen has worked as a solo pastor at a small church, an associate pastor at a medium-sized church, and is now senior pastor at a 650-member Presbyterian church. The solo pastor position afforded her a great deal of solitude, as she was often the only person in the office during the week. But she reports that her associate position was more suited for an extrovert, because it was program driven and required her to be constantly out among people, especially in the never-ending work of recruiting volunteers. That was why, when her current church recently called an associate pastor, Karen suggested that they find an extrovert to partner with her. Out of all these positions, Karen prefers the senior-pastor position because people expect her, as the weekly preacher, to spend a good deal of time studying and writing. As the chief administrator and supervisor, she is often removed from the center of the action and is able to invest in the development of other staff members and elders.

I was surprised to discover that many senior pastors of large churches are introverts. I had assumed that the more people in a church, the more extroverted the pastors needed to be. In fact, introverts can thrive in these positions because, in large churches, people do not expect their senior pastor to be as accessible, and the model of leadership tends toward training and coaching rather than the more traditional roles of pastoring and counseling. Head pastors of large churches, instead of spreading themselves thinly and superficially among the throngs of the community, can devote themselves to the development of other leaders who can then distribute themselves among the constituency of the church.

LEADING DIFFERENT TYPES OF PEOPLE
Leading extroverts. It's easy to forget, as we as introverts are learning to relish the depths of our own temperament, that there are extroverts out there who find us utterly alien. The authors of *Type*

Talk at Work observe that "As is the case with all Introverts, an Introverted leader has a lot brewing under the surface, but only lets out or shares a small piece of it."[16] This can be deeply mysterious to extroverts, and they can view this internalizing tendency with suspicion. When we take a moment for quiet, they may consider us to be withholding from them. Or they may interpret our silence in a brainstorming conversation as either rejection of or assent to their ideas. They may even mistake our natural reflectiveness to be apathy or indecisiveness.

With that in mind, perhaps the most significant aspect of successful leadership is communication, as we cannot lead others or compel them to follow a vision if we cannot communicate with them. This is especially true when working with people who do not speak the language of "introvert." A consistent critique of my ministry has been a lack of communication. What people sometimes consider to be my flaws betrays their extroverted expectations for communication. For extroverts, it is natural to regularly talk over ideas with people, to check in often and to seek feedback, but for introverts, these things require conscious, consistent effort. Introverts are prone to thinking and acting very independently. Our temptation is toward isolation from others, but Christian leadership and life is always characterized by interdependence. So introverts need to discipline themselves to depend on others and to seek their input.

Over-communication. An indispensable instrument in the toolbox of an introverted leader is "over-communication." The "over" in this strategy will only be perceived by introverts; to extroverts this is just "communication." Aware of our proclivity for enigmatic silence, introverted leaders act in love and understanding toward extroverts when we practice communication that is unnatural to us: we give more feedback and affirmation than we think is necessary; we repeat ourselves, even several times when making an important point; we contort our faces and gesticulate; and we sometimes give expression to incomplete thoughts to let extroverts know that we're engaged in the conversation.

Education. As an introverted leader, I have to do more work educating people about my personality type than do extroverted leaders. I've done this in a variety of settings—in the pulpit, in leadership meetings, in pastoral interactions and in casual conversations. I've found that even a little explanation about what life is like as an introvert goes a long way in dispelling myths and establishing understanding. This is helpful both for extroverts to begin to understand introverts, and also for introverts who will find their experience normalized by interacting with leaders who are like them. I've been encouraged that the communities I have been a part of have been eager to embrace the different ways God has created us, and they value, both intrinsically and practically, that diversity. When I have explained to these communities the nature of introversion—why I need time to myself, what I enjoy, what I struggle with, and what my silence does and does not indicate—they have been appreciative and empathic. The most gratifying Christian community experience I have had was when, after modeling confidence in my introversion and leading extensive conversations about different personality types, introverts came to be celebrated as equally as extroverts.

Leading introverts. Though leading introverts should come more naturally to us, sometimes we spend so much time in the world and language of extroverts that we neglect the introverts among us! One of the most important things I have learned about leading my fellow introverts is that I need to give them the space to speak. Part of my role as a leader of a community is to carve out speaking room for those who do not normally do the talking but who have incredible insight to offer. My ministry colleague Mark, who has done a lot of work in group dynamics, observed that most meetings are dominated by a few assertive, usually extroverted, speakers. An entire meeting can pass with only two or three voices being heard. Most introverts, and less assertive extroverts, will not try to compete with or interrupt a steady flow of words. Mark is particularly troubled that meetings are the places where decisions are made and that the verdicts are largely determined by the outspoken minority.

What can we do to encourage introverts to speak, without putting them on the spot or imposing undue pressure on them? One simple thing we can do is give people a meeting agenda several days before a meeting, so that those who need to think before they speak will have the opportunity for prior consideration. In the meeting itself, we should establish ground rules for group discussion. We need to be clear that we are not only here to give our opinions but also to listen to one another, so it's bad form to interrupt one another.

The most fruitful strategy that I have employed has been inserting personal reflection time into a meeting. When an important decision needs to be made, I have given people time to step outside of the room and consider their individual opinions. When introverts have had time to process internally, they will be more likely to share their thoughts in the group. When a group is on the verge of a highly significant, ministry-shaping decision, Mark will separate the meeting into two days, so that people will have time to reflect in between meetings.

When I lead Bible studies, I will give everyone time to work through the text and consider their questions privately before I open it up to group discussion. I will usually go from person to person and have them list their individual questions so that everyone has a chance to contribute. Depending on the person, in the middle of a discussion, I might call on someone who has not previously spoken. This strategy requires caution and, usually, a relationship with that person and a knowledge of his or her comfort level in group interaction. It is also critical that a leader not call on people until sufficient discussion has taken place, so that introverts will have had time to entertain their opinions and formulate their thoughts. It involves some tact on the part of the leader so that people interpret your requests as an invitation, not as a demand.

AN EFFECTIVE INTROVERTED LEADER

Steve has been the pastor of La Verne Heights Presbyterian Church, a three-hundred-member congregation in California's San Gabriel Valley, for fifteen years. As an introvert with a strong pastoring gift, if he were given the choice, he would spend the vast majority of his ministry in one-on-one interactions in his office, helping people discern the voice of God in their lives. He is surprisingly talkative for an introvert, even disposed to lengthy sermons, yet he has placed the discipline of listening at the center of his ministry. His sermons are marked by frequent, reflective pauses, and he has incorporated regular silences into worship services. When he prays, both in pastoral conversations and when leading worship, he will sit in silence for up to a minute before he ventures to speak. When he does speak, his words are gentle and full of feeling, and others often feel as though they are being enfolded into the embrace of God.

In 2003 Steve was diagnosed with multiple sclerosis, which prompted some searching questions about whether he should step down from his position. But, together, Steve and the congregation have restructured the nature of the church's ministry, using his crisis as an opportunity to create a more collaborative community. Once the weekly preacher, he is now part of a team of pastors and elders who shoulder the preaching responsibility, and the congregation has come to enjoy hearing different voices and perspectives on Scripture. Further, Steve has been able to narrow the scope of his ministry, and has enjoyed more freedom to exercise his pastoral gifts while enabling others to apply their gifts in teaching, administration and community building. Others have since mobilized to lead in mission and outreach, and the congregation has developed important ministries to impoverished, urban areas in Los Angeles. This atmosphere has enabled Steve to thrive as an introvert, embracing his rhythms of retreat and engagement, and focusing more time on his strengths. And the community he leads is healthy and faithful to the biblical picture of the church.

8

Introverted Evangelism

"The question I put to myself is not 'How many people have you spoken to about Christ this week?' but 'How many people have you listened to in Christ this week?'"

<small>EUGENE PETERSON, *THE CONTEMPLATIVE PASTOR*</small>

"An introverted evangelist? Isn't that an oxymoron?" was the response I received when I explained this chapter to a seventy-year-old hospice chaplain, who was, until that moment, known for her sensitivity and gentleness. If the juxtaposition of *introverted* and *evangelist* does indeed result in an oxymoron, then it owes not to an inherent contradiction but to a caricature, a culturally distorted understanding of evangelism. In all circles, Christian and non-Christian alike, the word *evangelism* has incredible power to conjure negative images, cringes, even guttural reactions. At its worst, the word is a window to images of hellfire-and-brimstone, street-corner preachers spouting off to passersby. Even at its best, *evangelism* summons pictures of animated extroverts armed with quick wit, apologetic skill and the gift of gab.

If introverts are the ones who write books about prayer, then extroverts have cornered the market in the evangelism aisle.

Typical evangelism books always seem to locate airplanes as the most advantageous setting for evangelistic encounters, where at 30,000 feet, restive unbelievers are unable to escape the advances of brash Christians. One of my most vivid, and discouraging, memories involving evangelism was set in an airplane en route from southern California to Seattle during my sophomore year of college. Headed home for Christmas break after finals week, I was feeling the triumphant wooziness of the previous evening's all-nighter before my constitutional law exam, but I was conscious enough to overhear the conversation in the row ahead of me. Seated there were two other college students on their way home; one was a student at a liberal arts college adjacent to mine, the other a student at a Christian college fifteen miles away. After a hasty introduction, the Christian student asked a question to the other student about his religious background, and before he had time to give much of a response, the Christian had launched into a rambling presentation of the gospel. He preached and testified his way through the two-and-a-half-hour flight, much to the chagrin of his fellow student who only managed a few sentence fragments during our soporific trip—not to mention everyone in the surrounding rows. As I disembarked from the plane, I remember drowsily praying "God, please don't let this interaction forever close this guy off from the gospel."

During that flight I had no inclination either to contribute to that conversation or to engage the person next to me in a spiritual conversation. Truthfully, most introverted Christians I know would be delighted to bless the evangelistic efforts of extroverts and return to their lives of solitude and contemplation with a sigh of relief. The irresolvable problem with that move is that the Bible consistently links evangelism with our general program of discipleship. We must constantly guard against a private understanding of faith. Our process of growth as followers of Jesus necessarily includes sharing the good news that he died to enact. Introverts do not receive an evangelism exemption.

In actuality, I do not think that introverts are ill-suited for evangelism; I think that our prevailing evangelistic methods are ill-suited for introverts. Don Everts, author of *Jesus with Dirty Feet,* wrote to me that in popular teaching about evangelism, "the unspoken message is that only a gregarious person who's naturally relational can be an effective witness, which overshadows the fact that we're *all* called to be a part of this wonderful adventure of evangelism." Rick Richardson, professor of evangelism at Wheaton College, says that our common image of an evangelist is a "spiritual salesman":

> Many Christians think they have to dump their content on someone and then close the deal, or else they haven't really shared their faith. This basic paradigm of evangelism as individuals seeking to make the close on a sales call permeates the evangelical consciousness. . . . This paradigm of evangelism is a barrier to Christians, for it leaves them feeling like they don't have a part to play in it. If they aren't extroverted, persuasive, an expert on their product, skilled at responding to the questions that will come up, and able to be pushy and assertive when it comes to making the close, then they don't identify with evangelism as part of their life and gifts.[1]

If evangelism is defined as cornering a stranger long enough to sell our product—present the full gospel and extract a decision—then "introverted evangelist" is destined to remain an oxymoron. We must move away from inauthentic interpretations of this central Christian discipline and learn how to reshape it and practice it as ourselves. I would like to present a different model of evangelism that is a better fit for introverts. Instead of a salesman peddling our spiritual wares, I propose that we explore mystery together.

EXPLORING MYSTERY TOGETHER

> O the depth of the riches and wisdom and knowledge of
> God! How unsearchable are his judgments and how inscru-
> table his ways!
>> "For who has known the mind of the Lord?
>>> Or who has been his counselor?"
>> "Or who has given a gift to him,
>>> to receive a gift in return?"
> For from him and through him and to him are all things.
> To him be the glory forever. Amen. (Rom 11:33-36)

> When I came to you, brothers and sisters, I did not come
> proclaiming the mystery of God to you in lofty words or wis-
> dom. For I decided to know nothing among you except Jesus
> Christ, and him crucified. And I came to you in weakness
> and in fear and in much trembling. (1 Cor 2:1-3)

The apostle Paul may have marveled at the surpassing, probing mysteries of God more than any other human being. He saw the fullness of God captured not in sonic booms of divine judgment or in raw displays of power but in Jesus hanging on a splintered Roman cross, the "failed" Messiah. Jesus' death and resurrection flung open the gates of salvation to all people and nations, inaugurating a new creation in a parched, withering world. The mystery of God is not a riddle to be solved through human ingenuity; it is a panoramic vista of indescribable beauty that reveals our own smallness and frailty. Paul understood that the only proper response to the revelation of such profound mystery is to tremble.

When it comes to the nature of God and the gospel of Jesus Christ, I'll always have more questions than answers. God has pulled back the curtain long enough for me to have glimpses, but the more I learn, the more expansive God's kingdom becomes. For too long we have envisioned evangelism as one person, carrying a quiver of answers, assaulting another person who is armed with the questions. Or in another image, the dividing line is between the person who stands at the summit and another who is trekking and slipping his way up the mountain. Rather, I consider us all to be explorers of the mysteries of God.

Fellow explorers are bound together by their trust and friendship, and by their shared aspirations and struggles. Our friendships with seekers involve a deepening process of intimacy and vulnerability. As our friendships develop, it is natural that conversations would turn to matters of ultimate meaning. Here is where the depth of introverts becomes an incredible asset in sharing the gospel. We are people who have gone deep into our souls, and we have insight into how God's power and love have reached the darkest parts of our lives. The gospel paradox is that when we reveal our own weaknesses, we come in touch, and put others in touch, with the One who has the ability to heal. Evangelism does not entail a relationship between strong and weak; it's a relationship of two people conscious of their limitations and wounds, drawing strength from God and from each other. Rick Richardson reflects that "as you develop genuine friendships you will probably be surprised by what your greatest asset is. It's your humanity. It's your weaknesses, doubts, and questions. Most people today are not at first interested in your answers. But they will immediately relate to and identify with your questions and struggles."[2]

In exploring the mysteries of God together, we relieve ourselves of the need to be the "expert." The formerly humiliating answer of "I don't know" becomes not only possible but even profound. Ronald Rolheiser asserts that "The contemplative believes that, since God is radically and totally other than ourselves and our reality, we can live patiently and believe in God, despite seemingly unanswerable paradoxes, and despite pain and injustice."[3] This mindset transforms awkward pauses into sacred silences, in which we wait for God's illumination.

As we explore mystery as fellow travelers, the tone of our conversations moves away from the conflict and debate that is so unpleasant for introverts. Too much evangelism is attempted out of defensiveness; someone charges Christians with being illogical, intolerant or hypocritical, so we rush to the defense and try to disprove their accusation. This creates a polemical environment that only pushes people further back into their corners. However, the verbal tool of exploring mystery together is not confrontation or preaching but dialogue. We subject ourselves to the same questions we pose to others, and as we traverse them together, we may arrive at surprising conclusions we could never have reached when simply trying to defeat one another's logic. Our questions are open ended, granting the other person the freedom to respond or not to respond. The questions stick with us, even haunt us, long after we ask them, and we await insight together. The process is more important than an immediate decision.

My understanding of evangelism shifted dramatically when I began to view my role not as initiating spiritual conversations but rather as responding to the ways that God is already at work in people around me. Introverts are more exhausted by initiating than by responding, but if we see evangelism as responding to God's prior work, we discover more energy and joy. Evangelism becomes about cultivating spiritual awareness and about discerning the subtle movements of the Holy Spirit in people we encounter.

I see my function less as walking people through a formula of faith and more as dropping spiritual hints. In the first method, I am the one who controls the conversation; in the second, I try to give glimpses of God and enable the person to respond to the promptings of the Spirit who is already at work. Jesus' teaching tool of choice was the parable, stories that worked from the basic realities of human existence—farming, soil, relationships, trees, debt, work—to give glimpses into the unsettling, subversive nature of God's kingdom. The parables, as sometimes understood,

were not earthy illustrations that shed light on otherwise inscrutable spiritual realities. In fact, they hid just as much as they illuminated, and they were tools that separated those genuinely seeking God from the religiously complacent, or merely curious. The
parables revealed the divide between these groups. Those who
were just entertainment seekers went away puzzled, but for those
who were earnestly seeking God, the parables became means for
further exploration and pursuit of Jesus.

George Hunter, professor of church growth and evangelism at
Asbury Seminary, says that in a postmodern culture, indirect and
imaginative approaches to evangelism have far greater potential
than a direct, logical style. He follows Kierkegaard in saying that
the direct approach often leads to conflict and defensiveness,
while a more subtle approach entices the imagination and engages
people on levels deeper than the rational level so featured in modern evangelism. Hunter cites Vincent Donovan, Catholic missionary to the Masai people of East Africa, who once "observed that
Protestant leaders seem to trust only the sense of hearing, and
therefore rely almost totally upon using the preached and taught
Word to reach and teach people. By contrast, Celtic Catholics believe that God can use all five sense to 'speak' to people."[4]

My former colleague Jennifer, a part-time college pastor and part-
time sculptor (and full-time introvert), sees her art as part of her
worship of God and also as a means for spiritual interaction. It's not
simply that her art becomes a conversation piece, which leads to
discussions about the gospel, but she believes her art itself to be a
wordless testimony to the beauty and majesty of God. She hopes
that as people experience her sculpture they experience God.

A quote commonly attributed to St. Francis of Assisi is "Preach
the gospel at all times—if necessary, use words." This line is not an
introverted license to stay silent about Jesus. Though our Christian
witness involves more than words, it never eliminates words altogether. But I am convinced that God's movements in our lives super-

sede words, and our attempts at speech are weak and clumsy transmitters of ineffable reality. Paul's assurance in Romans 8:26 that "the Spirit helps us in our weakness; for we do not know how to pray as we ought, but that very Spirit intercedes with sighs too deep for words" seems to say that the most searching communications, even those that occur in the throne room of God, move beyond words. As we seek to share the gospel, we must remind ourselves that the Spirit nudges and works in ways that defy explanation.

When I was a hospice chaplain, I regularly worked with people who had lost the ability to speak. They moved in and out of consciousness, but even when they were lucid, they could not talk. When I first began sitting at their bedsides, I felt useless. As a pastor, I made a living by using words, and if you took those away what else would I have? I felt like a mere observer, and I wished I had something more "practical" to offer these people, like the nurses did. But as I spent more time with these noncommunicative patients, I started to notice a fascinating pattern. When they neared death, they would raise their hands into the air, almost like they were being welcomed and embraced by someone in another dimension. It was as if they had feet in two separate realities: one in the present world and one in the world to come. I also noticed that when I sat with these people straddling the cracks of the universe, I would feel a powerful sense of peace wash over me. God was moving in invisible, confounding ways. When I would attempt to describe these things to others, my words felt hollow and trivial, like they were stripping those experiences of their mystery.

Through those interactions, I began to pray differently. When I prayed for people who I knew were not Christians, I prayed less that God would give me an opportunity to explain the gospel to them and more that God would be touching those places of their lives that only God can reach, that he would speak into those areas of their souls that can only comprehend God's voice. Author Rebecca Pippert proposes that "When we ask God to let people experience the love of Jesus through us, something happens that can't be quantified or easily explained. That's because prayer involves mysteries that happen to the soul."[5]

CONTEXT

Few introverts will argue against the idea that sharing the gospel is stressful and tiring, even when we have redefined evangelism in a way that suits introverts. We can help create more comfortable situations when we place ourselves in contexts that feel natural to us.

For most of my life, since I started taking my faith seriously, I was convinced that I was a feeble evangelist. This was not mere self-negation; I was *told* that I was weak in evangelism. During my years as a college pastor, two of my supervisors listed evangelism as the area requiring the most improvement. This was especially a high priority when I worked directly on a college campus, and I struggled to meet the expectations of the highly evangelistic organization. They envisioned me establishing relationships with non-Christian students on their own turf, pioneering Bible studies for seekers in dormitories and modeling for Christian students how to take people from unbelief to belief. Just trying to traverse the life disparity between myself—a thirty-year-old, married Christian from Generation X and an eighteen-year-old student from the Millennial generation who did not share my faith or worldview— was exhausting enough. I had little remaining energy or audacity to initiate significant spiritual conversations. My threshold for awkward social interactions was only so high. After a few fruitless attempts over the course of a semester, I stopped making efforts. It felt futile, draining and discouraging. While I could teach the value of evangelism—and my extroverted, evangelistically gifted staff partner would have me lead training sessions, because most students could not relate to *his* evangelism stories!—I lacked the drive and the passion to persevere.

After my ignominious showing as an evangelist in those days, I found myself as a chaplain ministering to terminally ill patients and their families. No one expected me to engage in evangelistic conversations, and in fact, "proselytizing" in that position was illegal. Yet day after I day I prayed for people who had no religious commitments. They welcomed me into their homes as someone who could listen and help bear their emotional burdens. Conversations easily turned toward questions about God and spirituality and life after death. Together we sat in pregnant silences and stood at the threshold of transcendent mysteries. One night I joined hands and prayed with a family as their father took and released his last breath, and we stood on holy ground.

Through experiences in these starkly different ministries, I learned that in college ministry I had been attempting evangelism in the wrong context. For who I am, and how I form relationships, hospice ministry was a comfortable environment for me to interact with unbelievers. This doesn't mean that introverts are disqualified for college ministry; another introvert I know is gifted in the ministry that I flailed in, helping college students reach a point of confession of faith. However, much of our evangelistic "success" is dependent on situating ourselves in contexts that match our temperaments, interests and gifts.

For introverts, the most natural setting for sharing the gospel will be one-on-one friendships. We don't need to drain our reserves searching far and wide for people who are asking spiritual questions. Instead, we ask who are the people who are *already* in our lives, and how is God at work in them? In our spiritual friendships we are free to be and share the gospel as ourselves. Pippert is adamant about this point: "Let God make you fully you. Rejoice in your God-given temperament and use it for God's purposes. This point cannot be emphasized enough. We must be authentic. If we try to be someone we are not, people will see it instantly."[6]

Authentic evangelism will involve applying the gifts we have as introverts to our spiritual friendships. For example, our acts of service demonstrate the radical servanthood of Jesus. Our perseverance and inner fortitude illustrate God's strength and faithfulness. Our compassion translates into a love for the poor and a commitment to God's justice. Our prayerfulness reveals a personal God that we can have relationship with and is tenderly involved in our lives. Again, we may find that our listening abilities are powerful tools in cultivating relationships and revealing the nature of God. We might even call our style of evangelism a "listening evangelism." When someone who identifies herself as a Christian truly listens to another person, it conveys the love and compassion of Jesus in ways that talking about that love never could. Eugene Peterson reflects on the nature of listening: "pastoral listening requires unhurried leisure, even if it's only for five minutes. Leisure is a quality of spirit, not a quantity of time. Only in that ambiance of leisure do persons know they are listened to with absolute seriousness, treated with dignity and importance."[7]

My evangelistic conversations these days resemble spiritual direction more than they do preaching. I ask questions and prayerfully listen, while acknowledging mystery and nudging the other person toward God. Because introverts process internally, we can offer a nonjudgmental posture and others will be comfortable opening up their lives to us. I had a friend tell me once that he felt like he could tell me anything at all—even that he was an alien from outer space—and my reaction would be "Huh. Tell me more about that."

Our gift of helping others slow down is important in our witness to the nature of God. Postmodern people are not as persuaded by rational argumentation as much as they are by a lifestyle that substantiates a person's worldview. If we want to be persuasive apologists in this culture, we need to invite people into a lifestyle that is different from the status quo. If we are advertising to a world, which is weighed down with busyness, that becoming a

Christian just involves adding more activities to your already-overloaded agenda, what is the appeal of the Christian life? Introverts who lead slower, unhurried, reflective lifestyles are very appealing representatives of the One who said "Come to me, all you that are weary and are carrying heavy burdens, and I will give you rest" (Mt 11:28).

Our spiritual friendships involve time, process and patience. Introverts, when committed to a particular relationship, may try to rush past what they consider to be superficial small talk and move directly into serious and intense conversation. But this will create an awkward environment and will short-circuit the normal progression of friendship that is so important for building trust. People are far less likely to let us into the vulnerable parts of their lives if we do not show an interest in *all* of their lives. So it is important to remember that friendships begin with sharing common interests, and a good place to start in evangelism is building relationships around your interests. Important questions to ask are what is it that I love to do, and how can I involve others in those things?[8] The benefits of this method, for introverts, are that in doing something we love, we gain energy, and since introverts talk most about things they have prior knowledge and experience with, it helps facilitate conversation.

There is another component of pursuing mutual interests that is more sublime. When we pursue those things we love, we delight in God and his gifts. God has engrained in all of us particular passions, drives and interests, and in pursuing them with a Godward perspective, we engage in worship. As worshipers, we have every reason to believe that God is deeply at work, not only in us but in the people around us, so when we are enjoying the gifts of God, we are attuned to the movements of the Spirit and more receptive to what, or who, God shows us.

In my early twenties, I acquired a taste for wine, an interest that has developed into a full-bodied passion for the winemaking process, as well as the culture and community that surrounds its cultivation. Living less than three hours from the vineyards that blanket the California central coast, my wife and I frequent the area on long weekends. I've been up there enough times that the people who work at the wineries we frequent know me by name and even know what types of wines I enjoy. I have an almost limitless capacity for discussing wine; my highly extroverted wife will be waiting in the car while I'm lingering to chat with winery employees and tasters.

Without intending it, I have found myself in several conversations about God while in wine country. At one winery hung a painting of two men carrying a large cluster of fruit between two poles, which I recognized as an artistic depiction of the Israelite spies returning from their reconnaissance of Canaan (Num 13:26). When I pointed that out, it led us into a spirited conversation about the Bible and religious faith, and one man left saying he would read the story of the Exodus and Israel's entry into the Promised Land. Furthermore, because wine in our culture carries the symbolism of romance and the good life, conversation easily moves into relationships, memories, regrets or losses. Conversations are aided by the fact that Scripture is saturated with images of grapes, vineyards and wine. Jesus illustrated the refinement of discipleship through vines and branches (Jn 15:1-8), he passed on a sacramental tradition that centers around bread and wine (Lk 22:17-20), and he turned jugs of water into the best wine the wedding guests had ever tasted (Jn 2:1-11).

If we look closely enough, we will find that there are echoes of grace in all of our interests. To look at our passions this way is to view the world sacramentally, a world that is teeming with outward signs of invisible realities. The connection between God and creation has been distorted by sin but the new creation inaugurated by Jesus' resurrection is reawakening hearts and minds to see the handiwork of the Creator. Music and art take us beyond the ordinariness of words and expose us to dimensions and levels of our humanness that words cannot touch. Reading and writing put us in the presence of ideas and insights that come from the mind of God. Team sports have an incredible power to bring people together and create a community spirit that transcends individual contributions. Outdoor activities take us to raw, unfiltered places of the world that show forth God's glory and reveal our fragility. Commitment to environmental stewardship and preservation points to a God who creates and is intimately involved in his creation. As we develop our friendships around our shared interests, we can use all of these symbols to point our friends to the God who is behind them.

PRACTICAL STEPS

Here are some suggestions for helping introverts thrive in evangelism:

1. *Narrow your focus.* Rather than scattering yourself, focus on building relationships with one or two people with whom you feel comfortable and who have displayed spiritual curiosity. Work in small steps.

2. *Ask questions.* Open-ended questions cultivate relationships, and at the right time, have the power to unlock people's deepest desires. Jesus would often respond to people's questions with another question, which forced them to account for their motivations and assumptions.

3. *Ask for time.* Introverts don't do as well when put on the spot. Instead of stuttering out an unprepared answer to a seeker's question, ask for time to think about it. "I don't know but I can find out" is a perfectly legitimate answer. Apart from evangelistic encounters, I will think about and formulate answers to some of the most common questions so that I will be ready when someone asks.

4. *Don't accept the premise.* West Wing chief of staff Leo McGarry taught his press secretary never to "accept the premise of

the question." Sometimes unbelievers will come at us with a hostile posture and ask us an accusatory question, like "How could you possibly believe in a God who would condemn people to hell?" If we accept the premise that God is a villain, we are put in a defensive stance and we let the other person control the conversation. Instead, rephrase the question. For example, you could respond, "Perhaps the real question is how could humans rebel against a God who created such a beautiful world?"

5. Find a comfortable environment. Consider participating in an Alpha class or in a Bible study for spiritual seekers. You could even start by joining an online forum for people with questions about God or creating a website designed for these sorts of discussions. Avoid debating situations that have no real goal other than disproving the opinions of others or just debating for debating's sake.

6. Know your role. You don't have to play every conceivable role in the great evangelistic task of the church. Focus on your strengths and what contributions you have to make to others. The best evangelism is done in community. We are part of a body of believers with different gifts and strengths—some have gifts of hospitality, others of service, others of teaching. A healthy community applies their gifts not only for the up-building of each other but also for the sake of those on the outside. Partner with other Christians (especially extroverts) in your relationships with unbelievers, and unbelievers will see the breadth and depth of the multifaceted love of God.

INTROVERTED SEEKERS

If introverts aren't persuaded that evangelism is an essential part of our discipleship, if they aren't convinced that they should wade into the extroverted waters of witness, or if they won't accept that there are introverted ways to share our faith, then perhaps they can be won over by one last claim: *introverted seekers need introverted evangelists.* It's not that extroverts can't communicate the gospel, either verbally or nonverbally, in ways that introverts finding appealing, it's that introverted seekers need to know and see that it's possible to lead the Christian life as themselves. It's imperative for them to understand that becoming a Christian is not tantamount with becoming an extrovert.

My most illuminating conversation about introverted evangelism was with Casey, an introvert who unnervingly found herself surrounded by a group of Christian women in college. When I met her, Casey had already gone through an extended process of conversion three years earlier, and she reflected on her journey toward faith in those years:

> Much as several extroverts played an important role in my coming to know God, it was definitely the introverts who, ironically, took center stage. The extroverted believers I knew primarily offered me a place in community, a social network that could provide me with something to do on Friday night. But for something as important as spirituality, I needed one-on-one conversations and someone who understood my need to sit and think on things. Introverts could monitor the level of my emotional fuel gauge and would give me space when I needed it. They offered me the chance to respond to the message by going off on my own to journal, rather than making some immediate statement or reply to a person (or worse, a group) without sufficient time to process. I found myself free to contemplate who Jesus was, rather than worry about people's expectations of me.

Introverted evangelists bear with their fellow introverts over time, understanding that faith is more of a process than a one-time decision. As their friendships become more intimate so do the questions. They meet introverted seekers in their depth of reflection, and they understand their rhythms of engagement and retreat, interaction and solitude. Introverted evangelists affirm that God embraces introverted seekers just as they are, and they demonstrate a life of following Jesus as an introverted disciple. As our culture grows in fascination with spirituality, introverted Christians can lead the way in introducing others to a personal spirituality rooted in relationship with the risen Jesus. Introverted seekers are hungry for introverted Christians to find the courage to live authentically and to witness to the God who created them as introverts.

9

Introverts in Church

"If an audience is not immersed in an aura of mystery and symbolic otherworldliness, then it is unlikely that it can call forth the state of mind required for a nontrivial religious experience."

NEIL POSTMAN, *AMUSING OURSELVES TO DEATH*

The first three-quarters of the sanctuary were occupied by people who had attended the church for years, stretching back to their days in Sunday school. Over the years the church settings had changed—from classroom to youth group room to traditional worship service to contemporary worship service and now the Sunday night postmodern worship gathering—but the seating arrangement had remained the same. They sat in their well-established groups of friends, as comfortable as they were in their own homes with their own families. In the last quarter of the room were a few rows of solitary stragglers, spaced out by an empty seat or two in between. These people were visitors or, in some cases, regulars who had not been attending since birth. They were drawn to worshiping God in a postmodern language that they understood, but they were wary of the rigid social boundaries.

At the time of Communion, the pastor said there would be an experimental new format for taking the sacrament. He explained that the Lord's Supper is not an individual act but a corporate meal in which we celebrate together the meaning of Jesus' death. Therefore, instead of coming up to the front one at a time to partake of the elements, people would come up in groups and celebrate Communion together. He instructed them to choose their own groups, from the people situated around them, and to assemble at the table when they were formed.

My friend Sarah, an introvert who attends frequently, sat in the second-to-last row. After hearing these directions, she stood up, in extreme social discomfort, and walked out of the sanctuary. Sarah is an ordained Presbyterian minister.

A 2006 article in *Christian Standard* presented this chilling scenario:

> Imagine hearing the following at the opening of your next church service:
>
> Welcome! We're going to worship the Lord in spirit and in truth today. So let's strip off all encumbrances by removing our shoes, socks, and accessories. Now, grab someone new and give them a hug. Go on, don't be shy. In fact, the Bible tells us to greet one another with a holy kiss! Now, empty out the contents of your pockets and purses and form small groups to examine them together. Open up to those around you. Tell them your fears and weaknesses so you can feel the love of your Christian family.[1]

And all the introverts cringed together.

Though the author obviously writes with hyperbole, her point is well grounded: the culture and practices of evangelical worship services can be painfully unpleasant for some people, even those who are wholeheartedly devoted to Christ and his mission. The familiarity and informality of some churches in the evangelical tradition, with their best intentions of devotion and hospitality, can actually *exclude* introverts. Times of greeting and sharing in a public context, especially with strangers or distant acquaintances, are unnatural and sometimes painfully uncomfortable. In fact, some introverts I interviewed conceded that they commonly show up late on Sundays to avoid the awkward preservice socializing and greeting times.

As part of my research, I attended several churches of varying denominations, sizes and worship styles—though most of them identified with the evangelical tradition. I visited a colossal mega-church with a professional and polished service, an alliterative three-point sermon, and an eye for seekers. I attended a small Quaker church, with a wall of windows behind the pulpit, which looked out on the San Gabriel mountains. I visited a traditional and echoing Episcopalian church, an evensong, a meditative Taize service, many contemporary services at carpeted Presbyterian churches, and three postmodern worship gatherings bursting at the seams with young people.

My most disappointing worship experience took place at a large church that has quadrupled in six years, their numbers swelled by college students and twentysomethings. At thirty, I was anticipating a service that communicated the gospel in a familiar language. We lined up at the door before the service started as if waiting for a bouncer to check our names off the list and open the velvet ropes. After getting cleared to enter, I sat down on my folding chair, where I was inundated with blaring music, flashing colored lights, floating images and rolling PowerPoint announcements on numerous screens around the room, and the loud chatter of young adults laughing and flirting. Clearly this was not a time for silent prayer. At the start of the service, the scream of the electric guitar caused everyone to leap out of his or her chair. For the next thirty minutes people clapped and danced and cheered their way through a frenetic worship set.

After an extended announcement time, the pastor preached a long message on sacrificial love. Fifty-five minutes of preaching later, I was already exhausted, and the service was only half over. After the sermon, however, I experienced a glimmer of hope. The lights dimmed, the screen went black, the guitar switched from electric to acoustic, and people bowed their heads. We would have a chance to sit with the Lord, praying, listening and resting in his presence. The worship leader explained what this time was for and gave some instructions for how to pray. After that he provided some suggestions for what to pray for. He repeated the refrain that started with "Maybe you're feeling": *Maybe you're feeling hopeless. Maybe you're feeling like God could never forgive you. Maybe you're feeling uncertain about what God wants for your life.* Then he proceeded to quote some biblical passages that address those feelings, God's words to those who are struggling. He went on to preach a minisermon that reassured us that, in Christ, our sins are forgiven, and after a two-second pause, the electric guitar sprung to life. We were up on our feet again celebrating. The entire two-and-a-half hours of worship was filled with a steady, pounding stream of words. And though there wasn't a false word uttered during the service, I left feeling empty and disoriented. Never have I needed a nap so badly after church.

A paradox I uncovered in my research is that introverts often feel more freedom in worship services that feature traditional liturgy than they do in ones that feature more open, informal, unstructured styles of worship. Introverts often appreciate the depth of liturgical prayers and hymns, as well as the rich symbolism that fill traditional churches. They may feel less expectation from worship leaders in these churches to offer outward, emotional responses. One friend who attends a traditional church said that the liturgy "guides me into God's presence" and requires less energy on his part than the nondenominational church he used to attend.

Some introverts decry the shallowness of contemporary worship songs and their repetitive refrains, which can feel emotionally manipulative. They say that loud music disrupts their internal dialogue with the Spirit. One member of a charismatic church lamented that when people showed emotion in worship, the pastor would proclaim "The Spirit is really moving this morning!" These kinds of churches tend to encourage spontaneous bodily responses—raising arms, kneeling, dancing—and many introverts are uncomfortable with these kinds of reactions and the attention they draw. And the more the expectation for this kind of worship grows, the more introverts consider it artificial and stifling.

I do not wish to reinforce introverted stereotypes that we are melancholics who are unable to have fun or celebrate, who spend our hours in self-important isolation and would prefer to live in a soundproof room lined by black walls. I consider myself an animated and socially confident introvert, who enjoys concerts and sporting events and even crowds in the right situations. The point is that when introverts enter into worship, we are apt to come trembling before a God whose mysterious otherness often reduces us to silent awe. For us, quiet is often the context for heartfelt worship. For centuries a "sanctuary" was not only a holy place for worship but also a safe harbor for refugees. When introverts go to church, we crave sanctuary in every sense of the word, as we flee from the disorienting distractions of twenty-first-century life. We desire to escape from superficial relationships, trivial communications and the constant noise that pervade our world, and find rest in the probing depths of God's love. We want to hear God's voice, which comes to us more often in whispers than in triumphant shouts.

The movement in the church toward "postmodern" expressions of worship, in my view, is an advantageous shift for introverts. Churches are moving away from worship environments that resemble the locales of our daily lives and are returning to the idea of a sanctuary as a holy place. Evangelicals are embracing ancient forms of liturgy and ritual, which include meditative prayer, silence, and imaginative and nonverbal worship expressions. We are rediscovering the power of symbols, which have the ability to eclipse the impact of all the words uttered in a service. The cross, once marginalized by "seeker services," has now returned to its place of prominence. Protestant churches, suspicious of icons since the Reformation, are bringing art and images into their sanctuaries, recognizing their ability to foster an atmosphere of prayerfulness and sacredness. We are learning to incorporate all human senses into our worship of God—not just the sense of hearing.

I've been a part of worship services that have people painting and sculpting during the service as their expression of worship. Some churches line their walls with art done by people in the congregation, which not only adorns their sanctuaries but communicates a sense of community that transcends chatting at the fellowship hour. In some cases, the bright lights and the dancing images on video screens have been supplanted by candles and stained glass images that tell the biblical story.

When I was a college pastor, we tried a number of different worship experiences that resonated with the introverted students. In a Good Friday service, we created prayer stations centering on different aspects of the meaning of Jesus' death: In one corner we placed a wooden cross and kneeling pillows. In another, we set a bowl of water so that the students could wash their hands as a symbol of God's cleansing effected through Jesus' death. At the front of the room, the students could write their sins on a piece of paper and nail them to another wooden cross. A fourth station featured Scripture passages for reflection, illuminated by candles. Another had pictures of people in impoverished parts of the world so that we could prayerfully embrace our role in alleviating the suffering of others. For the thirty minutes that the students moved through the stations, the only sound in the room was the haunting echo of hammers pounding sins to the cross.

My point here is not that churches should coddle introverts. I do not intend to create yet another target audience for a church culture that is already marinating in consumerism. We should not cater our worship services to introverts anymore than we should to extroverts. There are times when introverts *should* feel uncomfortable in worship, though we should be cautious as to the *degree* of discomfort. But if we are always comfortable, our faith goes stagnant.

Introverts need to be challenged to experience God in ways that stretch us, and we need to be in situations that help us grow in love for others. Introverts may need to keep struggling through greeting times in church, because we need the constant reminder that the Christian life is never lived in isolation. Roy, whom I mentioned in chapter five, startled me when he said that introverts actually play a critical role in welcoming others. Because introverts understand what it's like to be on the outside of a community looking in, we can relate to people who are visiting our church and extend hospitality to them in nonintimidating ways.

However, my hope is that churches will begin to recognize when their worship services are communicating to introverts that their ways of living and relating and worshiping are inferior or unfaithful. Just as there is not one shape of discipleship, there is not one mold of worship. I would like for my fellow pastors to understand that hourlong sermons may overwhelm a sizable demographic of their congregations, and a two second silence for personal confession may feel like a mere hand wave at people who want to interact with God in a quiet way. In fact, as we find more balance in our worship, it will not only be introverts who benefit. Extroverts too will learn to listen for God in the cracks of their speech and grow in understanding that "in quietness and in trust shall be your strength" (Is 30:15).

CHOOSING A CHURCH

Personality makeup is an important consideration in choosing a church. However, introversion is only one factor in finding a church environment that suits you; different types of introverts will feel at home in different sorts of churches. Many introverts, steeped in nuance, will appreciate that finding a church home is more complex than matching a church to a list of requirements— a strategy that works no better in searching for a church than it does in searching for a mate. We think we have a perfect image of the person who will suit us, only to find ourselves captivated by someone completely different. In the same way, churches have a way of choosing us, a process that is mysterious, sovereign.

The number and variety of churches in the United States tempt us to choose a church in which we feel completely comfortable, which requires no growth or movement on our part. If it is our aim, we can find a church that is the corporate reflection of our personality. If we consider evangelism distasteful, we can find a church that is silent on the topic. If we don't consider poverty and social justice to be part of the gospel agenda, then we will have no trouble finding a church that shares our opinion. If we introverts want a church that will allow us to be anonymous and isolated in our individual worship experience, we need not look far.

I remember an older gentleman who visited our church a few years ago; he became genuinely exasperated when four separate people introduced themselves to him before the service. He said he wanted to be invisible in worship. While I sympathize with this desire, and I acknowledge that there are various levels of community participation, I do not consider long-term anonymity to be a healthy form of belonging. What we celebrate in the Christian life is that we are *not* anonymous. We are intimately known by God, and our life in community should be an embodiment of that reality.

Further, if a community will not extend the hospitality of Jesus to us, but allows us to float in and out of worship like apparitions, then we will be hindered from engaging in the mission of God in and through that community. As we look for a church, we are not only searching for a comfortable home, we are searching for a body of believers in which we can serve and participate in God's kingdom project as ourselves. We want a church that both blesses our introversion and calls us to be disciples walking the way of the cross, which is the way of love for the world.

All that being said, introverts will often be attracted to churches that offer depth. Depending on other temperamental factors, some introverts will be drawn to churches that have a deep sense of spirituality and prayerfulness. They will want to see that people are devoted to personal and corporate spiritual disciplines and to the meditative reading of Scripture. One introverted friend said that she had chosen a Quaker church because of their emphasis on silence and waiting on God. However, other introverts will be pulled to communities that value creativity and the imagination, a church that understands that art and music are important forms of worship. Still other introverts will want a church that focuses on the life of the mind, in which ideas take a place of prominence. They will want a church that elevates scholarship and teaching and understands that a life of study can also be a life of devotion.

Most introverts told me that they appreciate churches that move at a slower, more thoughtful pace and do not equate the Christian life with manifold activity. My friend Kathy and her husband recently wrote to me about their reason for leaving their church:

> I realized we were mismatched with the vision our pastor had for the church, and he was not supportive of an introverted approach to the Christian life. It was not intentionally hurtful on his part, but he taught that those who are matur-

ing in Christ would participate in the activities he outlined. If you weren't doing those things, he would challenge you to take greater steps of faithfulness. The things he emphasized would come naturally to you if you were an extrovert, but might be uninteresting, distasteful or difficult if you were not. There was a sense that the more you surrendered to Christ and sought to grow in him, the more you would want to do all the things he recommended, like attending a weekly three-hour, cell-group meeting and joining mission trips with large groups of people. We knew there were many fine people in that church who were serving Christ in amazing ways. Since their activities often didn't fit the pastor's rubric, he was blind to the wonderful ways in which they were following Christ. To listen to him tell it, we were languishing in indifference.

The message that is delivered from the pulpit about the contributions and lifestyles of introverts is a significant factor for us to feel at home in a congregation.

Introverts often feel more comfortable when at least one of the pastors or other central leaders is also an introvert. My pastor is an introvert and, though he rarely discusses it in detail, his approach to the Christian life resonates with my own. When he preaches about evangelism, he emphasizes the importance of taking a personal and genuine interest in the people around us, one at a time. Every year he takes several personal prayer retreats, and he encourages others to do the same.

At the same time, extroverted pastors can also be very effective in leading introverts when they acknowledge the value of introversion, which is deeply validating. The critical question to ask is not *Do the leaders act like me?* Rather, it is *Do they affirm the variety of personalities, gifts and experiences in the Christian life, or do they try to conform people to a mold of faithfulness?*

WELCOMING INTROVERTS

Because many of the introverts in our communities of faith at times feel excluded and displaced, our churches would do well to take intentional steps to welcome introverts. I had many conversations with both introverts and extroverts about how our churches can reach out to introverts, and here are some of the best suggestions.

Celebrate differences. When churches publicly celebrate that there are different kinds of people in a community, it allows people to explore their lives of faith in authentic ways. Simply recognizing that there are introverts out there is a great place to start in validating them. Before the weekly greeting time, my pastor often acknowledges that not everyone is comfortable with this practice. Many knowingly nod their heads as he acknowledges that he is an introvert and he finds this part of the service a little awkward. But his example of commitment to an intimate Christian community motivates the rest of us to step beyond our comfort zones.

Even further, when gathered together for worship, the leadership can make it clear that people participate in different ways. Some will enjoy more outward displays of devotion and others will have a more inward experience. Some will be celebrative, others contemplative. Some will listen or pray when others sing. When churches acknowledge these differences, it frees people both to worship in their individual ways and also to try different forms of worship.

A church I worked at offered a regular class for helping people discover their unique gifts and passions, using a curriculum that assessed spiritual gifts and personality type. Largely because of this class, this church had a tremendous lay ministry, which included many introverts who were thriving in ministries that suited their individual gifts. At a Pentecostal church, a person I know said he appreciates the emphasis on spiritual gifts, because it affirms that each person has a valuable role to play in the church.

Additionally, sometimes it may be helpful to have introvert-specific gatherings. When I was a college pastor, my colleagues Lexie (an extrovert) and Audrey (an introvert) formed a group called "Faith and Friends," which was a small group designed for introverted types on the shy side, who had the desire to make relationships but not the social expertise for doing so. This group enabled introverts to find genuine community without having to navigate larger and more intimidating social gatherings, and it also gave them greater confidence in other settings. They met weekly and discussed books and different topics, and they slowly started sharing more of themselves with each other. Each week, in one-on-one contexts, they discussed open-ended questions such as "What is your family like?" and "What do you like the most/the least about Christian community?" I led a seminar on introverted leadership for them, and the format allowed these people to exercise their blossoming leadership gifts in ways they were not yet comfortable with in other settings.

Recalibrate leadership gauges. I am convinced that the most effective way to change a church culture is by calling different sorts of leaders. In chapter seven, I discussed how transformative it can be for introverts in a community to see other introverts in leadership. It is both validating and empowering for introverts to know that their personality traits do not disqualify them from leadership.

Introverts bring much-needed balance to a leadership team, so invite introverts into the various teams/committees in your church that deal with worship, education, leadership selection, evangelism and hospitality. Or teach the community about spiritual direction, and provide training for interested people. Or train people in the ministry of listening and the ministry of presence; the Stephen Ministry that is offered by many churches may be particularly appropriate for introverts, as it involves one-on-one relationships in which someone walks with, and listens to, another person in a time of pain or transition.

Finally, there are some important leadership questions that I think every church should ask itself: (1) "What are our measures for gauging leadership potential?" (2) "How do we identify and select our leaders?" (3) "Is our evaluative lens extroverted?" (4) "Do we exclusively look for charismatic, gregarious pastors?" (5) "How important is it that our leaders are skilled at *listening* as well as *talking?*" (6) "In selecting lay leaders do we elevate those who attend the most activities and are the most popular?" (7) "Or are we open to different kinds of leaders, people who are thoughtful and contemplative and who lead by example?"

Experiment with worship. There are elements that can be added to worship services that feed introverted souls. Find a way to insert authentic silences into worship. I say "authentic" because a brief perfunctory pause can feel like an empty gesture. Incorporate silences that last for several minutes, explaining their significance so that people will not think it's a mistake. One church I know allows a full two minutes of silence after every sermon. Simply inserting regular pauses in the content of worship services, instead of rushing from one component to the next, can also be fruitful. So much of our human relationships, even the very best parts, is unspoken, and our worship, in which we interact with a personal God, ought to reflect that.

Experiment with *lectio divina* and other contemplative forms of prayer and Scripture reading during church services. Find creative opportunities for wordless communication. Make symbols central. Appeal to the imagination. Create experiences that address senses other than hearing, such as the visual and the tactile. Incorporate art and prayer stations and acoustic music into worship. Give open-ended questions that leave introverts with things to chew on after they leave. Have components in worship that might make extroverts feel uncomfortable!

More sensitive introverts will find raucous services with loud music uncomfortable, and if this is the preferred music style of the church, at least provide some variety within the service. Better yet, offer different sorts of services (in addition to the regular Sunday services) that allow for quieter, smaller, more inconspicuous times of worship. Dan Kimball reports that "time and again I hear how important the darker environment is to those at our vintage-faith worship gathering. Attenders feel they can freely pray in a corner by themselves without feeling that everyone is staring at them."[2] One Presbyterian church I know with a "blended" style of worship on Sunday mornings offers an evensong service—a quieter, slower, liturgical service that often doesn't have a sermon—one Sunday night a month. Another Episcopalian church I have attended has a Taizé service once a month, a contemplative, candlelit worship service that originated in the Taizé community in France. If you choose to offer these types of services, make it clear that people are to go in in silence, as they are entering a holy place; this is not a time for socializing.

Reimagine programs and events. Prayer meetings may be the most important, and least attended, of all church structures. What's more, often the way they are set up is exclusive of the people in the congregation who are the most dedicated to prayer! There are few meetings I dread more than voluble, emotional, spontaneous and conversational public prayer meetings. So try different formats for prayer meetings, formats that are more inviting for introverts. Employ listening prayer and breath prayer or other creative and ancient approaches. Before we opened a new church building, I led a prayer meeting in which I had people prayerfully draw and write on pieces of paper that we posted on the walls. It was our reenactment of the drawing and carving that adorned the walls of Solomon's temple (1 Kings 6:29). I then asked them to picture the people that would be using that building, and who they would like to see worshiping in that building, and to silently pray for those people. After they had time to pray silently, we then closed with ten minutes of praying aloud.

Another way to help introverts get involved is to offer varying levels of participation. Introverts need the freedom to enter into and enjoy community in their own ways and at their own pace. So in large gatherings, place a few chairs and tables around the edges of the event, where people can have private conversations or rest while remaining in the room. Also provide smaller settings for interaction, in addition to big social events. Consider small groups that center around an activity or book discussion rather than ones explicitly focused on building relationships. Or experiment with different kinds of contemplative small groups, such as those that focus on listening prayer or group spiritual discernment. Provide training and resources for small groups, but do not require small group participation. Have termination dates for each small group, which will help introverts persevere through the awkward formation phase and also give them an opportunity to pull back and reflect when it has ended. Consider a church retreat that focuses on practicing spiritual disciplines or even have a silent retreat in which people are together in bonds of silence for twenty-four hours. Offer contemplative prayer classes, such as *lectio divina*. And provide behind-the-scenes service opportunities for introverts to employ their creativity and servant hearts.

Insert personal reflection times into meetings so that the introverts can process what they've heard and contribute to group decisions. Give everyone written agendas several days before meetings, and encourage people to send follow-up emails to the group with thoughts they have later. Offer programs that focus on the cultivation of the mind. Hold high-level Bible studies that look at Scripture in great depth, in their original cultural and historical contexts. Avoid using a biblical text as only a jumping-off point for personal and contemporary application. Give people homework and reading assignments. Bring in local scholars to teach theology, apologetics or church history classes.

Understand that technology is a mixed blessing. Technology in worship services can be a wonderful tool, especially as it provides a multisensory experience that speaks to many aspects of the human person. Churches are discovering how they can use technology to create a contemplative worship setting, to foster "sanctuary" in even the most mundane building. Once after I preached a sermon on the prodigal son, I projected Rembrandt's depiction of the parable onto a screen and gave people several minutes to silently reflect on it. The image was far more powerful than my sermon.

However, also beware that too many external stimuli can overload introverted filters and distract from our worship. Personally, I do not like a sermon outline projected behind the speaker, as I find it distracts rather than enhances. My brain is unable to follow both simultaneously. Finally, you might consider creating some online chat forums on the church website for introverts to interact with others and feel a part of the community.

●   ●   ●

When churches reach out to introverts, they not only offer healing to introverts but they heal themselves. Introverts have profound gifts to offer, and Christian communities benefit greatly from harnessing the power of introverts among their ranks. Introverts' thoughtfulness, spiritual depth, compassion and slower pace of life can be elixirs to those churches that have been poisoned by the superficiality, pragmatism and frenzied activity that marks our surrounding culture. When introverts and extroverts are mutually celebrated, not only in word but also in practice, both the depth of the church's ministry and the breadth of her witness are enhanced.

Finding Our Place

Our monastic ancestors retreated into solitude and found they were not alone. In the shifting sands of the desert, they discovered their place in the church. In contemporary Christianity, noise and activity threaten to stifle introverts, but we need to find our place, not only for our sake but for the sake of the church we love. The hurdles that introverts face are many, but the hopes we have for thriving are real.

In order to find our place in the church we must make two movements. We go into the desert, into the depths and riches of solitude, to listen for the whispers of God who created us as introverts and to discover the gifts we have been given. Through Christ we die to false identities and put away inauthentic behaviors. We honor the rhythms and practice the disciplines that give us life, energy and joy. We learn how to not only accept our temperaments but to relish and celebrate them.

The inward movement is not the end of the journey, though we will come back to it again and again. The other movement is toward others, toward community. We are not ultimately called to a life of self-fulfillment and comfort but to a life of love. We seek to love God and our neighbor as ourselves, knowing that genuine love comes out of who we are in Christ. We are to pass on the gifts we have been given. Sometimes we will use our words and other times we will model prayerful silence, reflective rest and compassionate listening. As we make this movement into community, we will find that it's not merely about us finding a place for ourselves, but it's about God showing us where we belong and the gifts we are to others.

Questions for Reflection and Discussion

Chapter 1: The Extroverted Church

1. How would you describe the personality of Jesus? If you are familiar with the Myers-Briggs Type Indicator, how would you categorize him?

2. Do you see the extroverted bias in your community of faith? Why or why not?

3. If evangelicalism values the doer over the thinker, what impact, whether positive or negative, do you think that has on the church?

4. If you are an introvert, how do you feel about the use of the phrase "introverted church" to describe a closed community that is only inwardly focused? What is another name you might offer instead for that distortion of the church?

5. What do you think about the decision of the monastics to retreat into the desert? Can you relate to that desire? What would be your motivation for finding that kind of solitude?

6. What positive changes do you think introverts could make in their churches? What assets do *you* have to offer your community?

Chapter 2: The Introverted Difference

1. Which dead European psychologist is a stronger force in your head, Sigmund Freud or Carl Jung?

2. What are the stereotypes about introverts that you face or hold?

3. If the three main attributes of introversion are (1) gaining energy in solitude, (2) processing internally and (3) preferring depth over breadth, then do you notice any of these patterns in your life? Is there one that is a stronger force than the others? Which attributes, if any, in the list on page 43 really describe you well?

4. What are your reactions to the section "Created as Introverts"? How does understanding the physiology of introversion affect how you view your temperament?

5. What do you think about the biblical figures that the author suggests were introverts? Are there others that you would add?

6. If it is true that God does not seek to conform people to a particular mold, but he works within their unique personalities and utilizes their individual gifts, both to bless them and others, do you find hope in that? Have you experienced that to be true in your life?

Chapter 3: Finding Healing

1. What messages did your family give you about introversion when you were growing up? Were they mostly positive or negative?

2. Do you relate to the stories of Lara and Mike? Are there things you do to overcompensate for the self-doubts or the limitations that you have?

3. Do the boundaries you draw with others tend to be overly

rigid or excessively flexible? Why do you think you tend in that direction?

4. Do you wrestle with shyness, social anxiety or depression? If so, how do you or can you seek healing?

5. If our ultimate identity is never found in aloneness, but it is found in relationship to another, then how do you let Jesus define you? How are you tempted to define yourself apart from Jesus?

6. What are the inward steps toward healing that you need to take? What outward steps can you take after some of the inward ones?

7. Have extroverts helped you find healing and discover your place in Christian community? If so, how have they done this? Are there people you can help find healing and affirm their contributions, and if so, how?

8. How can you grow in trusting God to work through you even when you are tired and empty?

Chapter 4: Introverted Spirituality

1. Saint Benedict said, "Because of the importance of silence, let permission to speak be seldom given to perfect disciples even for good and holy and edifying discourse." How do you respond to such a radical statement? Why would Benedict place such emphasis on silence?

2. What are some of the negative side effects that you see of our modern technology, in terms of disintegration?

3. What do you find appealing about contemplative spirituality?

4. If you feel that the world divides you from yourself, that you leave parts of yourself everywhere, losing yourself in the outer world, then what can you do to rediscover your sense of iden-

tity? How are you currently responding to that feeling of losing yourself?

5. What is the difference for you between privacy and solitude? How can you seek to practice true solitude? What distracts you from doing so?

6. What are the larger and smaller rhythms in your life? How do you pay attention to the connection between your body and soul? Which rhythms would you like to place more emphasis on?

7. What are the disciplines discussed in this chapter that you would most like to practice? Why?

8. What are the elements you would include in a rule of life? Take time to consider the questions on page 81. How would you like to structure your daily and weekly life so as to find joy, energy, and love for God and others?

Chapter 5: Introverted Community and Relationships

1. Do you relate to the author's lament that, though there is a universal desire to know and be known, his knowing is more intellectual than emotional? How so?

2. How are you challenged by the discussion about the Bible's emphasis on community? How are you tempted to give in to the individualistic viewpoint of our culture?

3. What is your church's understanding of belonging and participation? Do you agree with these definitions? What does faithful participation in a community look like to you?

4. Have you observed the pattern of the "introverted spiral" in your life? How have you or do you react to your desire to spiral out of community for a time? How have others responded to that pattern? How do you react to others' desire to spiral out of community?

5. Which one(s) of the gifts of introverts in community do you think describes you? Which of them would you like to cultivate? How can you use them, or other gifts you bring, to bless others?

6. Which of the suggestions for getting involved in community do you find the most helpful? What are practical steps you can take to build relationships and feel more a part of your community?

7. If asking questions helps cultivate relationships, what are questions you liked to be asked? Consider compiling a list of good questions that will help you get to know others on a deeper level.

8. Which of the "relational pitfalls" (enmeshment and one-directional relationships) do you most relate to? What steps can you take to develop healthier relationships?

9. How do you respond to conflict? Where do you think your reactions to conflict come from? What can you do to deal with conflict in a godly and constructive way?

10. What are the ways technology is a negative force in your life? What are the ways you can use technology to deepen your relationships and the contributions you make to others?

Chapter 6: The Ability to Lead

1. What do you look for in a leader? What does your church look for in its leaders?

2. Why do you think American culture exalts extroverted leaders? Do you agree that extroverts make better leaders?

3. What do you think about the list of expectations for pastors on pages 118-19? Do you have unrealistic expectations for what your pastor can accomplish? How can you help alleviate some of the pressure your community places on its leaders?

4. Do you think "Level 5 Leadership" is proving to be more effective than traditional models of leadership? Why or why not?

5. What stands out to you in the passages that discuss leadership, found in Titus, 1 Timothy and 1 Peter? What challenges you in those leadership descriptions? How can you become that kind of person and leader?

6. How do you think "the learning organization" and "sensemaking" open doors to introverted leaders? Are there ways you can incorporate those disciplines into your leadership or help your church practice those things?

7. What stands out to you in the examples of Mother Teresa, Martin Luther King Jr. and Jonathan Edwards? Is there one of them that you would like to learn more about? Do you have other introverted heroes of faith? Who are they, and why are they your heroes?

Chapter 7: Leading as Ourselves

1. If you were in Moses' position, how do you think you would have responded to God's call? Would you have protested or accepted the task?

2. Do you think that introverted leaders are tempted to hide? If so, what do you hide behind?

3. If you have served in a leadership capacity, do you think there is a cost that introverts pay in ministry? What has helped you to persevere? How can you grow in ministering out of God's power rather than your own?

4. Have you been intentional about self-care in your ministry? What are some important steps of self-care you have taken? What elements of self-care have you neglected?

5. Do you enjoy or dread preaching or public speaking? What are your strengths and weaknesses in this area?

6. Do you think that leaders should show their vulnerabilities as well as their strengths with people they lead? Why or why not? What have leaders modeled for you?

7. Do you find it to be true that the ministry of spiritual direction fits with the natural gifts of introverts? What about it do you find it appealing?

8. Have you seen or practiced models of leadership that focus on equipping others to do the ministry of the church? What are the advantages and disadvantages of such a system?

9. Does your church practice team leadership? What leadership roles and positions do you find most natural and life-giving? What about partnering with extroverts do you find to be exciting or intimidating?

10. Other than the things mentioned in the questions above, is there something else in this chapter that you found to be most important? How can you implement whatever you found to be most important into your life and leadership?

Chapter 8: Introverted Evangelism

1. What is your immediate reaction to the word *evangelism?* What images does it conjure?

2. Are you motivated to witness to your faith? What keeps you from talking to others about Jesus?

3. What are the strengths and weaknesses you see in the strategy of "exploring mystery together"?

4. Does the idea of "dropping spiritual hints" relieve some of the pressure you feel? What are some imaginative ways that you can point others toward God, while trusting that ultimately God is the one drawing others to faith?

5. What is the most comfortable context for you to have spiritual conversations? The most uncomfortable?

6. What do you think unbelievers appreciate (or would appreciate) about you? How can you use those gifts to reveal the nature of God?

7. What are interests that you have? How can you share those with others, thus creating fruitful opportunities for spiritual conversations?

8. How do you react to the idea that "introverted seekers need introverted evangelists"? How does Casey's story motivate you to share your faith with fellow introverts?

Chapter 9: Introverts in Church

1. Do the worship services at your church feel introvert-friendly? Which aspects feel welcoming, and which aspects feel foreign and uncomfortable?

2. Does the statement that many introverts feel freer with traditional liturgy than they do with contemporary forms of worship resonate with your experience? Why or why not?

3. Are there elements of worship you have not appreciated that you would now like to explore, even if they challenge you to grow out of your comfort zone?

4. Do you agree that introverts can play a critical role in welcoming others, because we know what it's like to be on the outside? How can you reach out to newcomers, in a way that's true to who you are?

5. Why did you choose the church you attend? Was your decision related to your temperament? In what ways are you tempted to participate in a community that simply mirrors your personality type and doesn't require you to stretch?

6. What messages about introversion and introverted ways of living and worshiping are conveyed in your church? Does your

pastor acknowledge there are different ways a person can lead the Christian life and still be faithful?

7. How can the strengths of introverts be transformative influences in your community?

8. How can you help your church make positive changes that will be embracing and affirming for introverts? How can you advocate for your fellow introverted believers?

Further Reading

Community and Relationships

Bonhoeffer, Dietrich. *Life Together.* New York: HarperOne, 1978.

Lamb, Richard. *The Pursuit of God in the Company of Friends.* Downers Grove, Ill.: InterVarsity Press, 2003.

Myers, Joseph. *The Search to Belong: Rethinking Intimacy, Community, and Small Groups.* Grand Rapids: Zondervan, 2003.

Ortberg, John. *Everybody's Normal Till You Get to Know Them.* Grand Rapids: Zondervan, 2003.

Evangelism

Bechtle, Mike. *Evangelism for the Rest of Us: Sharing Christ Within Your Personality Style.* Grand Rapids: Baker Books, 2006.

Pippert, Rebecca Manley. *Out of the Salt Shaker and into the World: Evangelism as a Way of Life.* Downers Grove, Ill.: InterVarsity Press, 1999.

Richardson, Rick. *Reimagining Evangelism: Inviting Friends on a Spiritual Journey.* Downers Grove, Ill.: InterVarsity Press, 2006.

General Personality Type

Keirsey, David. *Please Understand Me II: Temperament, Character, Intelligence.* Del Mar, Calif.: Prometheus Nemesis Book Company, 1998.

Kroeger, Otto, and Jane M. Thuesen. *Type Talk: The 16 Personality Types That Determine How We Live, Love, and Work.* New York: Dell Publishing, 1989.

Myers, Isabel Briggs. *Gifts Differing: Understanding Personality Type.* Mountain View: Davies-Black Publishing, 1995.

Introversion

Cain, Susan. *Quiet! The Power of Introverts in a World That Can't Stop Talking.* New York: Crown Publishing Group, forthcoming.

Helgoe, Laurie A. *Introvert Power.* Naperville: Sourcebooks, 2008.

Laney, Marti Olsen. *The Introvert Advantage.* New York: Workman Publishing, 2002.

Leadership

Barna, George. *The Power of Team Leadership: Achieving Success Through Shared Responsibility.* Colorado Springs: WaterBrook Press, 2001.

Collins, Jim. *Good to Great: Why Some Companies Make the Leap . . . and Others Don't.* New York: HarperCollins, 2001.

Jackson, Anne. *Mad Church Disease: Overcoming the Burnout Epidemic.* Grand Rapids: Zondervan, 2009.

Kahnweiler, Jennifer B. *The Introverted Leader: Building on Your Quiet Strength.* San Francisco: Berrett-Koehler, 2009.

Nouwen, Henri J. M. *In the Name of Jesus: Reflections on Christian Leadership.* New York: Crossroad Publishing Company, 1992.

Oswald, Roy M., and Otto Kroeger. *Personality Type and Religious Leadership.* Herndon, Va.: Alban Institute, 1988.

Memoirs by Introverted Authors

Lamott, Anne. *Traveling Mercies: Some Thoughts on Faith.* New York: Anchor Books, 2000.

Miller, Donald. *Blue Like Jazz: Nonreligious Thoughts on Christian*

Spirituality. Nashville: Thomas Nelson, 2003.

Winner, Lauren. *Girl Meets God: On the Path to Spiritual Life.* Colorado Springs: Shaw, 2004.

Spiritual Direction

Bakke, Jeannette A. *Holy Invitations.* Grand Rapids: Baker Books, 2000.

Benner, David G. *Sacred Companions: The Gift of Spiritual Friendship and Direction.* Downers Grove, Ill.: InterVarsity Press, 2004.

Peterson, Eugene H. *The Contemplative Pastor: Returning to the Art of Spiritual Direction.* Grand Rapids: Eerdmans, 1993.

Spirituality

Barton, Ruth Haley. *Sacred Rhythms: Arranging Our Lives for Spiritual Transformation.* Downers Grove, Ill.: InterVarsity Press, 2006.

Calhoun, Adele Ahlberg. *Spiritual Disciplines Handbook: Practices That Transform Us.* Downers Grove, Ill.: InterVarsity Press, 2005.

Dawn, Marva J. *Keeping the Sabbath Wholly: Ceasing, Resting, Embracing, Feasting.* Grand Rapids: Eerdmans, 1989.

Foster, Richard J. *Streams of Living Water: Celebrating the Great Traditions of Christian Faith.* New York: HarperOne, 2001.

Goldsmith, Malcom. *Knowing Me, Knowing God: Exploring Your Spirituality with Myers-Briggs.* Grand Rapids: Baker Books, 2000.

Nouwen, Henri J. M. *The Way of the Heart: Desert Spirituality and Contemporary Ministry.* New York: HarperCollins, 1991.

Notes

Chapter 1: The Extroverted Church

[1]Susan Howell, "Students' Perceptions of Jesus' Personality as Assessed by Jungian-Type Inventories," Journal of Psychology and Theology 32, no. 1 (2004): 50-58.

[2]Marti Olsen Laney, *The Introvert Advantage* (New York: Workman Publishing, 2002), p. 54.

[3]David Myers, *The Pursuit of Happiness* (New York: Harper, 1993), quoted in Marti Olsen Laney, *The Introvert Advantage* (New York: Workman Publishing, 2002), p. 6.

[4]Jonathan Rauch, "Caring for Your Introvert," *The Atlantic*, March 2003 <www.the atlantic.com/doc/200303/rauch>.

[5]Alan L. Hammer and C. R. Martin, *Estimated Frequencies of the Types in the United States Population*, 3rd ed. (Gainesville, Fla.: Center for Applications of Psychological Type, 2003). Also Laurie Helgoe, *Introvert Power* (Naperville, Ill.: Sourcebooks, 2008), p. xxi.

[6]In this book, I make sweeping observations about American culture and evangelical church culture, and these observations will not apply to every culture or church. Some world cultures are more accommodating to introverted values and have more room for introverts in leadership and group dynamics, just as some church traditions may feel more welcoming to many introverts. See Helgoe, *Introvert Power,* pp. 57-64 for a discussion about Japanese culture and introversion.

[7]Richard Beck, home page "A Walk with William James, Part 8: Introverts in the *Imago Dei?*" June 19, 2007 <http://experimentaltheology.blogspot.com/2007/06/walk-with-william-james-part-8.html>.

[8]IgnatiusInsight.com, "Thomas Howard and the Kindly Light," October 2004 <www.ignatiusinsight.com/features/thoward_intrvw_oct04.asp>.

[9]Mark Noll, *The Rise of Evangelicalism* (Downers Grove, Ill.: InterVarsity Press, 2003), p. 89.

[10]See chapter 6 for more on Jonathan Edwards.

[11]Os Guinness, *Fit Bodies, Fat Minds* (Grand Rapids: Baker Books, 1994), p. 38.

[12]Ibid., p. 56.

[13]Henri Nouwen, *The Way of the Heart: Desert Spirituality and Contemporary Ministry*

(New York: HarperCollins, 1991), p. 54.

[14]Mark Noll, *The Scandal of the Evangelical Mind* (Grand Rapids: Eerdmans, 1994), p. 12.

[15]Eugene Peterson, *The Contemplative Pastor* (Grand Rapids: Eerdmans, 1989), p. 49.

[16]See chapter 4 for more on contemplative spirituality.

[17]John Stott, "The Lord Christ Is a Missionary Christ," Urbana Missions Conference address, 1976 <www.urbana.org/articles/urbana-76-speeches-and-stories>.

[18]Richard Halverson, *The Timelessness of Jesus Christ* (Ventura: Regal Books, 1982), pp. 98-99.

[19]C. John Miller, *Outgrowing the Ingrown Church* (Grand Rapids: Zondervan, 1986), p. 33.

[20]Eddie Gibbs, *LeadershipNext* (Downers Grove, Ill.: InterVarsity Press, 2005), p. 84.

Chapter 2: The Introverted Difference

[1]See Marti Olsen Laney, *The Introvert Advantage* (New York: Workman Publishing, 2002); and Laurie Helgoe, *Introvert Power* (Naperville, Ill.: Sourcebooks, 2008), for more insight on the nature of introversion from two seasoned psychologists.

[2]The other pairs are intuition (N) and sensing (S), thinking (T) and feeling (F), and perceiving (P) and judging (J).

[3]Helgoe, *Introvert Power,* p. xxi.

[4]Otto Kroeger, Janet M. Thuesen and Hile Rutledge, *Type Talk at Work* (New York: Dell Publishing, 2002) p. 11.

[5]I have taken these three categories out of Laney, *The Introvert Advantage,* pp. 19-35.

[6]Kroger, Thuesen and Rutledge, *Type Talk at Work,* p. 97.

[7]This list taken partially taken from Laney, *Introvert Advantage,* pp. 29-30, and from the Virginia Association for the Gifted Newsletter (Fall 1999) <http://vagifted.org/index.htm>.

[8]This section draws in large part from Laney, *Introvert Advantage,* pp. 61-94; and Debra L. Johnson, John S. Wiebe, Sherri M. Gold, Nancy C. Andreasen, Richard D. Hichwa, G. Leonard Watkins and Laura L. Boles Ponto, "Cerebral Blood Flow and Personality: A Positron Emission Tomography Study," *American Journal of Psychiatry* 156, February 1999, pp. 252-57.

[9]Laney, *Introvert Advantage,* p. 69.

[10]Ibid., p. 71.

[11]See the very helpful chart in Laney, *Introvert Advantage,* pp. 84-85.

[12]The ironic thing is that the majority of the gifted are introverts, and 75 percent of the people with IQs over 160 are introverted. See Lesley Sword, "The Gifted Introvert" Talent Development Resources page, 2002 <http://talentdevelop.com/articles/GiftIntrov.html>.

Chapter 3: Finding Healing

[1]Marti Olsen Laney, *The Introvert Advantage* (New York: Workman Publishing, 2002), p. 53.

[2]Laurie Helgoe, *Introvert Power* (Naperville, Ill.: Sourcebooks, 2008), p. 10.

[3]Ibid., p. 226.

[4]Earle C. Page, *Following Your Spiritual Path* (Gainsville, Fla.: Center for Applications of Psychological Type, 1982), handout.

[5]Dietrch Bonhoeffer, *Life Together* (New York: Harper & Row, 1954), p. 23.

[6]Thanks to my friends Lexie Keller and Jonny Eveleth for the beginnings of these biblical insights.

Chapter 4: Introverted Spirituality

[1]St. Benedict, "Of Silence," chapter 6 of *The Rule of St. Benedict,* 1949 ed., trans. Rev. Boniface Verheyen, O.S.B. (Atchison, Kansas).

[2]Henri Nouwen,*The Way of the Heart: Desert Spirituality and Contemporary Ministry* (New York: HarperCollins, 1991), p. 45.

[3]Ibid., p. 46.

[4]Nicholar Carr, "Is Google Making Us Stupid?" *The Atlantic,* July/August 2008, p. 57.

[5]These two paragraphs were adapted from a blog post that I wrote on my Unresolved Tensions site, which is no longer active. Adam S. McHugh, home page, "Cell Phones and Disintegration," August 6, 2007.

[6]Roy M. Oswald and Otto Kroeger, *Personality Type and Religious Leadership* (Herndon, Va.: Alban Institute, 1988), p. 108.

[7]Ronald Rolheiser, *The Shattered Lantern: Rediscovering a Felt Presence of God* (New York: Crossroad Publishing, 2004), p. 23.

[8]Nouwen, *Way of the Heart,* p. 26.

[9]See chapter 7 for more about monthly and yearly rhythms that introverts can practice.

[10]Jeannette A. Bakke, *Holy Invitations* (Grand Rapids: Baker, 2000), pp. 22-23.

[11]See Shane Claiborne and Jonathan Wilson-Hartgove, *Becoming the Answer to Our Prayers* (Downers Grove, Ill.: InterVarsity Press, 2008).

[12]All quotes about St. Patrick are from Thomas Cahill, *How the Irish Saved Civilization* (New York: Anchor Books, 1996), pp. 101-19.

Chapter 5: Introverted Community and Relationships

[1]See N. T. Wright, *Jesus and the Victory of God* (Minneapolis: Fortress, 1996), pp. 274-78.

[2]Joseph Myers, *The Search to Belong: Rethinking Intimacy, Community, and Small Groups* (Grand Rapids: Zondervan, 2003), p. 16.

[3]Henri Nouwen, *The Way of the Heart: Desert Spirituality and Contemporary Ministry* (New York: HarperCollins, 1991), p. 53.

[4]Ibid., pp. 53-54.

[5]Meyers, *The Search to Belong,* p. 43.

[6]Nouwen, *The Way of the Heart,* pp. 33-34.

[7]Marti Olsen Laney, *The Introvert Advantage* (New York: Workman Publishing, 2002), p. 9.

[8]Paul D. Stanley and J. Robert Clinton, *Connecting: The Mentoring Relationships You Need to Succeed in Life* (Colorado Springs: NavPress, 1992), p. 41.

[9]Otto Kroeger, Janet M. Thuesen and Hile Rutledge, *Type Talk at Work* (New York: Dell Publishing, 2002), p. 147.

[10]Archibald Hart, *Coping with Depression in the Ministry and Other Helping Professions* (Nashville: W Publishing, 1984), p. 148.

[11]Eddie Gibbs, *LeadershipNext* (Downers Grove, Ill.: InterVarsity Press, 2005), p. 144.

[12]Shane Hipps, at Mars Hill Bible Church, Grand Rapids, Mich., in sermon titled "The

Spirituality of the Cell Phone," March 30, 2008.

Chapter 6: The Ability to Lead
[1]Marti Olsen Laney, *The Introvert Advantage* (New York: Workman Publishing, 2002), p. 54.

[2]Leonard Holmes, "Great Presidents Are Stubborn and Disagreeable," About.com page, September 4, 2000 <http://mentalhealth.about.com/library/weekly/aa090400a.htm>.

[3]Richard Daft, *The Leadership Experience,* 2nd ed. (Mason, Ohio: South-Wester, 2002), p. 122.

[4]Mary Evertz, "Charm Takes Over in Tampa," *St. Petersburg Times,* November 11, 1999 <http://sptimes.com/News/111199/JFK/Kennedy_charisma_over.shtml>.

[5]Daft, *Leadership Experience,* p. 18.

[6]Wilfred H. Drath and Charles J. Palus, *Making Common Sense: Leadership as Meaning-making in a Community of Practice* (Greensboro, N.C.: Center for Creative Leadership, 1994), p. 5.

[7]J. Oswald Sanders, *Spiritual Leadership* (Chicago: Moody Press, 1967), p. 71.

[8]Rick Warren, *The Purpose Driven Church* (Grand Rapids: Zondervan, 1995), p. 213.

[9]Roy M. Oswald and Otto Kroeger, *Personality Type and Religious Leadership* (Herndon, Va.: Alban Institute, 1988) p. 28.

[10]George Barna, *The Power of Team Leadership* (Colorado Springs: WaterBrook Press, 2001), p. 4.

[11]Ibid., p. 5.

[12]Jim Collins, *Good to Great and the Social Sectors* (New York: HarperCollins, 2005), p. 11.

[13]Paul Tokunaga applies the level-5-leadership paradigm to emerging Asian leaders, whose traits and values often parallel introverted characteristics. See Paul Tokunaga, *Invitation to Lead* (Downers Grove, Ill.: InterVarsity Press, 2003), pp. 138-48.

[14]Jim Collins, *Good to Great* (New York: HarperCollins, 2001), p. 39.

[15]Ibid., p. 38.

[16]Peter F. Drucker, *The Essential Drucker* (New York: HarperCollins, 2001), p. 269.

[17]Peter Senge, *The Fifth Discipline* (New York: Currency Books, 1990).

[18]Chris Argyris, "Teaching Smart People How to Learn," *Harvard Business Review,* May-June 1991, pp. 5-6.

[19]Drath and Palus, *Making Common Sense,* p. 5.

[20]Ibid., p. 4.

[21]Scott Cormode, *Making Spiritual Sense: Christian Leaders as Spiritual Interpreters* (Nashville: Abingdon, 2006), p. 11.

[22]Daft, *Leadership Experience,* p. 140.

[23]Elaine Aron, *The Highly Sensitive Person* (New York: Broadway Books, 1996), p. 18. Aron speaks not directly of introverts but of "highly sensitive people." The highly sensitive label will not fit every introvert, but there is significant overlap between the two categories.

[24]Del Jones, "Not All Successful CEOs are Extroverts," *USA Today,* June 7, 2006 <www.usatoday.com/money/companies/management/2006-06-06-shy-ceo-usat_x.htm>.

[25]Barna Group, "Pastors Feel Confident in Ministry, but Many Struggle in their Interaction with Others," July 10, 2006 <www.barna.org/FlexPage.aspx?Page=BarnaUpdate&BarnaUpdateID=242>.

[26]David Wood, " 'The Best Life': Eugene Peterson on Pastoral Ministry," *The Christian Century*, March 13, 2002 <http://findarticles.com/p/articles/mi_m1058/is_6_119/ai_84434057>.

[27]Barbara Brown Taylor, *An Altar in the World: A Geography of Faith* (New York: Harper-Collins, 2009), p. 88.

[28]Tobin Perry, "Erwin McManus and Family: On Mission Together," *HomeLife*, December 2006 <http://legacy.pastors.com/RWMT/article.asp?ID=312&ArtID=10573>.

[29]Fred Peatross, "A Conversation with Brian McLaren," *Wineskins*, September-December 2006 <www.wineskins.org/filter.asp?SID=2&co_key=1256>

[30]Christianbook.com interview with Donald Miller <www.christianbook.com/Christian/Books/cms_content?page=704162&event=AFF>.

[31]Brian Kolodiejchuk, ed., *Mother Teresa: Come Be My Light* (New York: Doubleday, 2007), p. 65.

[32]Keirsey.com lists Teresa as an ISFJ in "About 4 Temperaments: The Guardians," <www.keirsey.com/handler.aspx?s=keirsey&f=fourtemps&tab=2&c=overview>.

[33]Kolodiejchuk, *Mother Teresa*, p. 77.

[34]Ibid., p. 20.

[35]Ibid., p. 164.

[36]David J. Garrow, *Bearing the Cross* (New York: Quill, 1999), p. 37.

[37]Ibid., p. 41.

[38]Time.com, "Attack on the Conscience," *Time*, February 18, 1957 <www.time.com/time/magazine/article/0,9171,809103-1,00.html>.

[39]Garrow, *Bearing the Cross*, p. 58.

[40]John Gillies, *Historical Collections of Accounts of Revival* (Edinburgh: Banner of Truth, 1981), p. 352.

[41]Jonathan Edwards, Memoirs, from *The Works of Jonathan Edwards, Vol. 1* (Edinburgh: Banner of Truth, 1834), p. xxxix.

[42]Quoted in John Piper, *God's Passion for His Glory* (Wheaton, Ill.: Crossway Books, 1998), p. 44.

[43]John E. Smith, Harry S. Stout and Kenneth P. Minkema, eds., *A Jonathan Edwards Reader* (New Haven, Conn.: Yale University Press, 1995), p. 293.

Chapter 7: Leading as Ourselves

[1]Roy M. Oswald and Otto Kroeger, *Personality Type and Religious Leadership* (Herndon, Va.: Alban Institute, 1988), p. 30.

[2]Ibid., p. 31.

[3]Brian Kolodiejchuk, ed., *Mother Teresa: Come Be My Light* (New York: Doubleday, 2007), p. 74.

[4]Archibald Hart, *Coping with Depression in the Ministry and Other Helping Professions* (Nashville: W Publishing, 1984), p. 18.

[5]For the record, I slightly favor perceiving to judging in MBTI.

[6]Henri Nouwen, *Reaching Out: The Three Movements of the Spiritual Life* (New York: Doubleday, 1975), p. 52.

[7]Marti Olsen Laney, *The Introvert Advantage* (New York: Workman Publishing, 2002), p. 69.

[8]David Day, Jeff Astley and Leslie J. Francis, eds., *Reader on Preaching: Making Connections* (Surrey, U.K.: Ashgate Publishing, 2005), p. 272.

[9]Ibid., p. 267.

[10]My thinking about this topic was sharpened by Shane Hipps's book, *The Hidden Power of Electronic Culture* (Grand Rapids: Zondervan, 2005).

[11]Henri Nouwen, *The Way of the Heart: Desert Spirituality and Contemporary Ministry* (New York: HarperCollins, 1991), p. 63.

[12]Jeannette A. Bakke, *Holy Invitations* (Grand Rapids: Baker, 2000), p. 19.

[13]Mark Yaconelli, *Contemplative Youth Ministry: Practice the Presence of Jesus* (Grand Rapids: Zondervan, 2006).

[14]George Barna, *The Power of Team Leadership* (Colorado Springs: WaterBrook Press, 2001), p. 71.

[15]Ibid., p. 71.

[16]Otto Kroeger, Janet M. Thuesen and Hile Rutledge, *Type Talk at Work* (New York: Dell Publishing, 2002), p. 96.

Chapter 8: Introverted Evangelism

[1]Rick Richardson, *Reimagining Evangelism* (Downers Grove, Ill.: InterVarsity Press, 2006), p. 17.

[2]Ibid., p. 69.

[3]Ronald Rolheiser, *The Shattered Lantern: Rediscovering a Felt Presence of God* (New York: Crossroad Publishing, 2004), p. 55.

[4]George G. Hunter III, *The Celtic Way of Evangelism* (Nashville: Abingdon, 2000), p. 74.

[5]Rebecca Manley Pippert, *Out of the Saltshaker and Into the World* (Downers Grove, Ill.: InterVarsity Press, 1999), pp. 110-11.

[6]Ibid., p. 109.

[7]Eugene Peterson, *The Contemplative Pastor* (Grand Rapids: Eerdmans, 1989), p. 21.

[8]Richardson, *Reimagining Evangelism,* p. 68.

Chapter 9: Introverts in Church

[1]Mandy Smith, "The 'IN' Crowd: Ministering with Introverts in Mind," *Christian Standard*, June 29, 2006 <www.christianstandard.com/articledisplay_preview.asp?id=213>.

[2]Dan Kimball, *The Emerging Church* (Grand Rapids: Zondervan, 2003), p. 136.